KT-453-928

Fieldwork in Industrial Archaeology

J. Kenneth Major

CHESTER COLLEGE

ACC. No.	DEPT.	X
78/1594		

CLASS No.

609   MAJ

LIBRARY

B. T. Batsford Ltd *London and Sydney*

© J. Kenneth Major 1975
First published 1975

ISBN 0 7134 2928 3 (hardcover)
ISBN 0 7134 2929 1 (limp)

Filmset by Tradespools Ltd, Frome, Somerset
Printed by The Anchor Press Ltd, Tiptree, Essex
for the Publishers B. T. Batsford Ltd
4 Fitzhardinge Street, London W1H 0AH
B. T. Batsford (Australia) Pty Ltd
23 Cross Street, PO Box 586, Brookvale, NSW 2100 Australia

Contents

The illustrations

1 The tower of Brakspear's Brewery at Henley-on-Thames

Introduction

This book has been written for all those who wish to study the techniques of fieldwork in industrial archaeology. It is hoped that it will prove as useful for the student who is working on the subject of industrial archaeology full time as for the person who can only work on it in his spare time. There is a place for both the professional and the amateur in this relatively new discipline. Fieldwork must play a large part in this discipline because the recording of industrial monuments must attempt to cover the losses, through demolition or re-development, which are proceeding at an ever-increasing rate. Although this volume deals with work in the field carried out by industrial archaeologists, it must be remembered that the mere recording of the 'dead' monument is not enough. The processes which went on in these buildings and the people who worked on the machines and ran the factories are all part of the industrial archaeologist's brief for his studies. It is perhaps unfortunate that the emphasis on fieldwork which exists in the discipline at present cannot be relaxed. The research necessary to cover processes and personnel is something which must take second place when buildings are threatened with demolition. This volume is, therefore, a guide book for the industrial archaeologist who is working in the field and it is hoped that it will help him to improve his skill and to avoid some of the pitfalls.

The author, who is by profession an architect, became an industrial archaeologist in his spare time because of his love for windmills and water-mills, and because he had been working on a few watermills in a professional capacity at the end of the 1950s. Growing out of that specialization he has become more and more concerned to record the whole range of the industrial units in his own area.

In the preparation of this book the author has been assisted by several enthusiasts who have given him a broader insight into the needs of the subject. The author wishes to acknowledge an especial debt to Rex Wailes, Angus Buchanan and Lawrence Cameron for the training and help they have given. Thanks are given to Mr and Mrs Lee, for their permission to use the work on Dowrich Mill, and to the other owners of industrial monuments for the facilities they have granted to the author when he has worked on their property.

The author wishes to thank his wife, Helen, who, in addition to being an experienced fieldworker, is also an able typist and a harsh critic of his work.

1. The scope of fieldwork in industrial archaeology

The discipline of industrial archaeology is relatively new and the guidelines for its study are only beginning to emerge clearly. Obviously industrial archaeology has been practised for some time under the guise of local history. However, local history implies an archival approach to the activities of a locality and it lacks the 'gum-boot' approach which is essential to the industrial archaeologist. Professor W. G. Hoskins, in his approach to local history, insisted that the local historian must get out in his heavy boots to walk the area he was studying. The industrial archaeologist must also get out into the field, to find all the information which is apparent in the sites with which he is concerned, before he can complete his studies in the local archives. It is not much good, for example, to be able to quote, from an auction catalogue about a corn mill, its size and its capability, without also knowing what remains on site and how this can be related to the description in the catalogue. The site could well have been one which was frequently starved of water or subjected to severe flooding, things which would make quite a difference to the analysis of the usefulness of the mill.

When the worker first becomes involved in industrial archaeology he may be presented with a bewildering range of objects for his study. When the discipline first came into being and its first guidelines were being defined there were six categories for study: (1) Coal and metals; (2) Power; (3) Textiles, pottery and glass, food preparation, brewing and distilling; (4) Transport; (5) Building materials; and (6) Agricultural industry. Since the early days of the subject, three further and logical extensions of the original categories have been added: (7) Housing for industrial workers; (8) Public services; and (9) The industry of recreation. The last item is one which was seriously questioned as being worthy of inclusion but, in *The Industrial Archaeology of the Isle of Man,* this received good treatment in the study of hotels and boarding houses. As a result of this it can be said that the nine categories have now gained acceptance.

The guidelines of date for the discipline have been argued about and no firm conclusion has been arrived at for a starting or finishing date for the period covered by the discipline. To some, the stone axe factory on Stickle Pike in Westmorland is a valid starting point. Here, in the sixteenth century BC, a pocket of green stone was discovered which provided material for fashioning into superb axes. The axes were roughed out on the spot and then polished a little distance away before being exported all over the British Isles. Since the site was clearly a factory for trade it is deemed worthy of inclusion in the scope of industrial archaeology. Others would claim that the middle of the eighteenth century was the start of the Industrial Revolution and therefore the start of the period to be studied as industrial archaeology. This would be wrong because it would leave out the growth of canals and river navigations in the seventeenth century and exclude almost the whole of the Sussex iron industry which was a main source of iron for a long time in this country. For most workers, the 1914–18 war is defined as the stopping point for industrial archaeology but this would leave out the study of the aircraft industry, the film industry, electric power production and many other industries. With the present acceleration of inventiveness some industries come into being and then change again in the course of a decade. A lot of industrial archaeological fieldwork will have to be done on the up-to-date elements of our industrial pattern: power stations, nuclear reactors, container terminals and the like. The discipline can, therefore, be said to have wide boundaries.

The fieldworker in industrial archaeology will have several propositions for the use of his experience put to him. Personal inclination or external pressures may dictate where his fieldwork experience can best be deployed. The most useful study of all is that of the remains of an industry in a chosen area. An example of this is a county survey of brickworks. The fieldworker is often called on to make an emergency study of an industrial unit which is about to be demolished or gutted of its machinery. Ideally, however, the fieldworker may have the opportunity and the time to study an industrial unit in depth while the plant is still at work and when there is no immediate threat of demolition. To some, the most rewarding fieldwork is that done on an industry long since destroyed, where the powers of observation and deduction have to be brought into play to discover, let us say, the waterways serving waterwheel sites in an area such as that of the copper mines of the Coniston Massif in Lancashire.

The broad headings given in the first paragraph of this chapter are now extended and analysed to give the fieldworker some idea of the areas in which work can be carried out.

Coal and metals

Coal and other metals have been exploited in Britain since before the arrival of the Romans. There is some evidence of medieval coalmining throughout the Midlands and in the coalfields of Yorkshire, Durham and Northumberland. Bell pits were sunk through the upper strata into the coal measures. These were shafts which opened out at the foot so that the coal could be removed from the seams and the roof was not supported. As soon as the roof became unsafe, a further bell pit was opened up and the previous one abandoned. The flint mines at Grimes' Graves in Thetford Chase are a good example of bell pits, although they were used for mining flint and not coal. Iron was also mined in a similar fashion. Bell pits could only deal with coal which was within a reasonable ladder climb of the surface. By the early eighteenth century coal pits had begun to go deeper and were then in the form of vertical shafts which served horizontal passages running through the coal measures. As the depths of the mines increased it became necessary to raise coal mechanically and drainage became a problem. This led to the introduction of horse engines for winding and then to the first steam engines, first for pumping and later for winding.

Later methods of coalmining can still be seen on our coalfields, although in many cases the drive to recover the value of the scrap leads to the demolition of the pit-head gear, the corrugated-iron screening shed and the washing plant almost as soon as the pit is closed. The wonderful iron pit-head gears need to be recorded, for with the abandonment of steam engines for winding, the form of the pit-head gear has changed. With steam-engine winding, the large pulleys in the head gear were supported by stout girders running back to the winding house. Now, with electric hoist motors, the winding can be done directly over the shaft and so the shafts are crowned not by a lattice framework but by a concrete cylinder with the winding gear in a room on the top.

In examining a coal mine the fieldworker must not forget the other elements that went to make up the mine complex. The various types of waste tips derive from the different methods of transporting the waste. In some mines the waste was taken out on railway trucks to form an embankment and in others a special truck was taken up an incline and tipped out at the top to form an ever-increasing cone. There was a third type, in which a cable carried the trucks on a continuous route, and, at a pre-selected point, an arrester tripped the trucks upside down in turn so that the waste dropped to the ground. Even without evidence of rails or cable the shape of the tip can still indicate the method of disposal. Pit-head baths are an important element of the social scene. In the old days, changing rooms had rows of chains over pulleys in the ceiling and the miner hoisted his 'going home' clothes up to the ceiling and locked them there with a padlock on the chain. In the modern 'Dudok-type' bath house, clothing is kept in lockers as in any other industrial plant. Small communities of pitmen's cottages were built— sometimes at the pit head and sometimes a distance away—to serve several shafts under one ownership. The interlacing paths by which the miners walked to work are also an interesting point of study. Whilst coming more appropriately under the heading of transport, the staithes and coal drops on canals and at harbours are important elements of the mining industry's past and are being destroyed because coal is no longer transported by barge or boat but by lorry or rail. Finding these staithes and coal drops and the wagonways which served them can be a useful piece of associated fieldwork.

Mining for metals in Britain has now almost completely ceased and, except for the large opencast mining areas in the Midlands and a few tin mines in Cornwall, fieldwork on the metal sites is almost all the recording of past activity. The metal mines are usually in mountainous areas such as Cornwall, Somerset, Wales, Derbyshire, Cumbria, Yorkshire, Durham and Northumberland, so fieldwork on these sites can often be undertaken and enjoyed as part of a holiday.

There are still visible remains of Roman mining to be seen in mid-Wales and on the Mendips. In terms of fieldwork these can easily be sought out and investigated. Conventional archaeological techniques will be needed for most of the exploration of Roman mining fields. The remains of the activities of the Elizabethan miners can also still be seen. There is a worked-out vein at Simon's Nick which stands above the Lever's Water dam in the Coniston Massif. The remains of the smelt mill at Brigham near Keswick still exist, and this smelt mill was founded by the Mines Royal which brought German mining experts to this country in the Elizabethan period. There is evidence in many places of the seventeenth- and eighteenth-century mining of lead, copper and plumbago, but it is the nineteenth-century exploitation of these minerals which has left the greatest wealth of material remains. The reason for this is that there was no gradual decline in the production of metal from natural ore in Great Britain but rather an abrupt end. This meant that the sites were complete when abandoned, and so they have not been cannibalized to equip other sites.

Plate 2 shows the main sites in the Coniston Massif where the two valleys containing Red Dell Beck and Lever's Water Beck come together to form Church Beck which pours over the shelf of the hanging valley into Coniston itself. The main water supply comes from two tarns which have been increased in size by dams—Low Water and Lever's Water—and further water came from Red Dell Beck by means of a small weir. Whilst the whole area is dotted with shafts and levels (or adits), it is in the water supply and various dressing works that the greatest interest lies for the industrial archaeologist. Water was taken from one valley to the other by means of

2   The copper mine sites in the Coniston Massif in North Lancashire

clay-lined leats to provide additional power to waterwheels and to the various machines in the mineral dressing works. Red Dell Beck, on the right-hand side of the illustration, was dammed to supply water to a small dressing works which originally had two waterwheels. This became disused and the leat was extended to assist in driving the great haulage wheel which worked the trucks on an incline going up to the Bonser Level. The other water used for this came from Lever's Water Beck by means of a leat which was fed from a weir below the main falls about 30m (100 ft) below Lever's Water. Below this waterfall stood Paddy End dressing works which was fed by the Low Water Beck, Lever's Water Beck and Red Dell Beck. There was at least 800m (half a mile) of leat required to feed this site. The remains of the waterwheels, the wheel pits and the water supplies enable the fieldworker to determine their size and their power. Whilst the Coniston area with its coppermines is well documented, there are many less well-known areas of mines and mineral dressing works up and down the country which would be very rewarding studies for the fieldworker.

Iron was mined extensively in certain parts of Britain and the high-grade iron-ore (haematite) mine at Hodbarrow in south Cumberland closed as recently as 1968. The remains there are gradually being obliterated by the influx of water in the areas of subsidence and by the demolition of the mine buildings and the associated steelworks at Millom. All around the Furness district of Lancashire there are bloomeries where the primitive smelting of iron took place. These are very early smelting furnaces where iron was made. Plate 3 shows the furnace at Duddon on the Cumberland bank of the river Duddon. There is, however, more in the remains at Duddon than just

3   The Duddon furnace in Cumbria

the furnace. There were barns for the storage of ore and charcoal, stables, offices and housing. Work still needs to be done to survey the waterwheel arrangements which drove the blowing engines for the tuyères. Later steel- and iron-working sites still exist although most of those dating from the nineteenth century have gone. The iron-making sites at Wellingborough, which were large, have now all been demolished, and the site is an industrial estate.

Although the fieldwork for Robert Clough's book, *Lead Smelting Mills of the Yorkshire Dales,* was completed some 20 years ago, this is a model of recording. At that time the area had been worked out for some 50 years but the remains were still quite extensive. He was able to interpret his finds in the buildings by reference to documents and to reconstruct a great deal of the mechanism in his drawings. Similar areas of lead, copper and tin workings need to be treated to the same extent. Although the remains may not be as extensive as they were when Robert Clough carried out his field- work, they are worthy of the same amount of careful study.

Power

Power sources in all their various forms are possibly the most attractive areas for study in the field. Workers seem to gravitate towards the study of windmills and watermills without any prompting. This is because mills frequently exist in good country and also because the site has usually not been required for a different use—a fate which awaits other forms of in- dustrial plant.

Whilst a lot of people have been studying watermills, their wheels and their machinery, no real study has been made of the design of weirs and leats and other methods of delivering water to the waterwheel. The relationship between the design of waterwheels and the water supply in any given situation has, as yet, received little attention. Throughout the country as a whole there has been very little study of the regional variations in the design of millwork or the work of local millwrights. The later stages of mill construction with waterwheels by designers like Casement or Fair- burn have not been studied in detail. The water power used for textile mills, whilst it played a great part in the siting of the original mills, was replaced quite early by steam power and this has meant that the waterwheels have been lost. A great deal can be learnt from the empty wheel pits and water courses which can be related to the various stages in the growth of the industrial mills.

Windmills have better records deriving from fieldwork than almost any other industrial monuments and this is largely owing to the 50 years of

4   The wind engine built by John Wallis Titt at Crux Easton in
Hampshire

fieldwork which has been carried out by Rex Wailes. The results of this
work have been published in *The English Windmill* and in many papers
given to the Newcomen Society. However, one area of study which merits
the attention of the industrial archaeologist is that of the wind engine—
the annular sailed mill in which blades of corrugated iron or canvas form a
complete circle. These mills, of which there are a surprising number of
variants, are disappearing at an alarming rate. The ever-increasing concern
over the shortage of fuel may result in the re-introduction of this type of
windmill for supplying water in the remoter parts of some farms. Plate *4*
shows the wind engine installed by John Wallis Titt at Crux Easton in
Hampshire in 1893. This ground corn in the adjacent building as well as
pumping water.

   One area of natural power which requires a great deal of fieldwork is that
of animal-powered engines. The commonest form of this in Britain is the
horse wheel which drove thrashing machines, turnip choppers and other

5   The horse wheel at Narr Lodge, Quernmore, Lancashire

farm machinery. In the northern counties the sites of these engines are marked by the roundhouses attached to barns. Unfortunately engines survive in only one or two of these buildings. Animal-powered machines also exist for other purposes. A cast-iron horse wheel was used for mine haulage outside a level on the east flank of Wetherlam in the Coniston Massif in north Lancashire. Two or three horse engines which drove corn mills survive. Plate 5 shows the horse wheel of a horse-driven corn mill attached to a tithe barn at Quernmore near Lancaster. A different form of animal engine exists in which a man or animal walks inside a vertical drum to operate a windlass to raise water, building materials, or trade goods on canals. A surprising number of these have been discovered and are described in *Water Raising by Animal Power* by Hugo Brunner and Kenneth Major and more must remain to be found.

The previous examples of natural power formerly existed in great numbers. Power from heat engines and other forms of fossil-fuelled engines was present in most manufacturing processes in the latter half of the nineteenth century but the destruction of these is almost more complete than that of the natural-powered examples.

In the late 1930s, Lancashire mill towns were dotted with large mills, and sometimes mines, surmounted by tall, and often decorative, chimneys. Each belched smoke and marked some form of steam engine which powered the machinery of the mill or the mine. Some engines have been preserved, others have been allowed to remain but the majority have been removed for scrap and to release the buildings they occupied for other uses. The delightful guide, *Steam Power, an Illustrated Guide,* by George Watkins and Frank Wightman lists the 50 basic types of steam engine and the enthusiastic fieldworker may find one in unexpected places. There is a fine, though not complete, single-cylinder steam engine by Lampitt of Banbury at Bloxham Grove. This drove a pair of millstones and a hoist as well as a pulley for other portable machines.

Another area in which a lot of fieldwork is needed is that of the recording of steam engines which pumped water for drinking-water supplies. Not only should the engines themselves be recorded, but also the engine houses, boiler rooms and the associated chimneys. The preserved steam engine at Ryhope near Sunderland is an excellent example of a fine engine, good brick buildings and a matching decorative chimney.

Many diesel engines and gas engines still exist and these need to be sought out and recorded. Farms often have diesel engines for pumping or for supplying power. They also exist in various forms to assist with the supply of electricity. The engine nicknamed 'Thumper' which belonged to the Post Office at Stony Stratford is a historical example of this. The original power station at Newbury in Berkshire, which started life as a water turbine-driven station, had a row of diesel generators which had been added to over a period of 40 years. A similar series of engines exists in the brewery at Henley for the generation of the brewery's own electricity but they are now out of use.

Manufacturing industries

This classification is a very broad one and can be used to cover the production of textiles, paper, pottery, glass, brewing and distilling.

Textile mills for making cotton, wool and linen goods exist all over Britain and date back to the late medieval period in some areas. The making of woollen cloth was originally a cottage industry in which each member of the family carried out some part of the process. Wool was delivered by the trader and the finished cloth was collected by the same trader on his next round. The knitting industry at Dent in Yorkshire, which carried on until this century is a similar example. People could always be seen knitting in almost every situation as they knew that their livelihood depended on it. By the middle of the eighteenth century the factory, where the workmen became employees and were no longer self-employed as they had been in the cottage-industry days, was beginning to be established.

The factories which were built by owners such as Arkwright at Cromford and Strutt at Derby were great engineering achievements with a good architectural form. The structure of these mills was a valuable contribution to the history of architecture. Even the first iron-framed factory, built as a flax-spinning mill by Charles Bage at Shrewsbury in 1796, is a monumental building. The fieldworker can seek out similar mills from that period onwards. Plate 6 shows the blanket mill at Rode, near Westbury in Wiltshire. This small mill was stone built and had wooden floors. The original water-wheel and the later turbine were still in place when the author made measured drawings of this mill. The large mills, with their imposing chimneys, which exist principally in the cotton areas of Lancashire and the wool area of Yorkshire have not yet been adequately recorded. Clearly they should be photographed and, if the original drawings do not exist in local archives, measured drawings should be made of typical examples. The town of Lancaster has a fine collection of mills, many of which are in use for the production of linoleum or its modern equivalent. Cotton and jute processing were staple industries in Lancaster and the range of mill buildings which remains reflects the various facets of these trades in their functional design.

Paper is a material which has been made in Britain for about 500 years. Its production is now a process carried on in large factories. However, the

6   The blanket mill at Rode near Westbury, Wiltshire

remains of an earlier form of the manufacture of paper can be seen in areas which had a clean water supply such as the Cotswolds or the High Wycombe valley in Buckinghamshire. The original paper-mill buildings and drying sheds can often be found, now usually converted to other uses. There are good examples of drying sheds at Paper Mill Cottages, Little Barrington, in Gloucestershire, and at Haughton Mill in Northumberland. These drying sheds can be distinguished by the vertical slats, which are shuttered, and by the rows of hooks inside on which cow-hair ropes were stretched. On these ropes the separate sheets of hand-made paper were dried. Plate 7 shows Rag Mill, Slaughterford, in Wiltshire, which had been abandoned prior to demolition when the photograph was taken. In this mill the rags were reduced to 'stuff'—that is the plain fibres held in suspension in water— which was then taken to the next mill down the valley of the Bye Brook where it was made into paper and then into paper bags. Rag Mill contained all the machinery necessary for the reduction of rags to 'stuff'. This machinery was the original plant put in during the 1890s by Bentley and Jackson of Bury. The waterwheel which drove it was still in place.

The present-day pottery industry bears little resemblance to the industry of the late nineteenth and early twentieth centuries. Stoke-on-Trent no

7   The paper mill, Rag Mill, Slaughterford, Wiltshire

longer has hundreds of smoking kilns on its skyline. Indeed the fieldworker would be hard put to it to find a bottle kiln for pottery firing anywhere. The ranges of buildings in which the clay was turned and then fired had a characteristic form: ranges of one- or two-storeyed sheds, with the bottle kilns projecting through the roof in the centre. Apart from the units of pottery buildings there are other industrial processes attached to the pottery trade which do not exist close to the kilns. There are the stone-grinding mills which exist in Cornwall and in the area around the Potteries. In Cornwall, the china stone was ground to a fine clay, washed and packed in factories which contained one building in which a waterwheel drove the grinding pans and in which the china clay was heated and cut into blocks. The stone-grinding mills, such as that preserved at Cheddleton in Stafford-shire, ground up flint which had previously been calcined in a kiln. The calcined flint was placed in a large circular grinding pan which was filled with water. The bottom of the pan was made of stone blocks from Welsh or Yorkshire chert. Four arms with wooden bars in the pan rotated and pushed further blocks of chert around the pan to grind the flint. The finely ground material was held in suspension in the water and the larger particles sank to the bottom. The suspended material was then passed to the drying-kiln floor where most of the moisture was evaporated. Whilst fieldwork has been done in the Staffordshire and Cornish stone-grinding areas, there is a great deal of work still to be done on the flint mills of the Tyne and its tributaries and those in Yorkshire and County Durham.

Glass was made at several places in England and Wales in the past. One of the best areas for glass-making was the Weald of Sussex where the plentiful supply of charcoal and of sand from Hambledon provided the basis of the industry. Now the remains of this glass-making can only be found by conventional archaeological excavation methods. The furnaces of this period were small domed mounds in which the glass was melted in clay crucibles. Later, glass-making was carried on in the coal-producing areas, so that there are remains at Newcastle-upon-Tyne, Catcliffe near Sheffield, Nailsea and Bristol. The most prominent feature of a glass-making site was the glass cone. This large cone of brick contained both the furnace and the area where the men worked and in which all stages of glass-making were carried out, from the first melting of the glass to the final annealing process. The glass-makers abandoned the use of glass cones about the middle of the nineteenth century. They were replaced by ordinary furnaces which melted the glass in a conventional fashion. The glass was then poured out in sheets to cool on cast-iron trays. After cooling it was polished between rotating heads with polishing powder. Sheet glass, polished glass and glassware are now made by machines in an almost automatic process. Fieldworkers can usefully trace glass-working sites and their associated buildings, because, apart from the measured drawings of the Catcliffe cone published in *Industrial Archaeology,* vol. II, no serious work has been done on these. No one, for instance, has done any serious work on the glass industry at Hartley in Northumberland or that at Leamington-on-Tyne.

Breweries and distilleries have distinctive buildings, except in cases in which modern processes of brewing have been adopted; breweries then look like any other factory. Until the nineteenth century, brewing was essentially a cottage industry. The local public house usually brewed enough beer for its own needs. The brewery behind the Wellington Arms at Stratfield Turgis in Hampshire (figs 5–7) is an example of the small privately operated brewery. This was gutted at a time when the creation of hotel bedrooms was encouraged by a government grant. Breweries of the next larger size still exist and trade. The brewery at Donnington in Gloucestershire is typical of these. Here the small brewery supplies 17 public houses and the process of making beer is the responsibility of a small group of dedicated workers. At the end of the nineteenth century each town had two or three breweries, each marked by its characteristic tower in which the beer was produced, passing from stage to stage down the tower. The Brakspear brewery at Henley (*frontispiece*) is a small example of this type of brewery and is still working. In a brewery like this one can still find steam engines and pumps—not necessarily in use—which were needed to move the liquor at various stages, to lift barrels and to generate electricity for the building. As steam was required for heating purposes during processing, steam engines continued to survive, only to be replaced by machinery powered by electricity in recent years.

Distilleries, although not quite so distinctive as breweries, still exist in Scotland in parallel forms, from small ones to those belonging to large combines.

Associated with brewing there are two types of buildings which are quite distinctive—but neither are necessarily attached to the breweries which they serve. The hop kilns of Kent, Sussex and Hereford consist of a two-storeyed barn to which square or circular kilns are attached. The pockets of undried hops are stored in the upper part of the building, spread out, and then placed in a thick layer on the upper floor of the kiln. Here the heat from an anthracite fire underneath slowly dries the hops. From the

8   A range of malt kilns, Sawbridgeworth, on the river Stort

drying stage they are taken back on to the first floor where they are poured down a hopper to be compressed back into hop pockets and stored before being taken to the breweries. Maltings are far larger and can vary considerably in design and detail. The body of the malting is often several storeys high, though floor to ceiling is often only 1·65m (5 ft 6 in.) or 1·80m (6 ft), and at one end there is a single kiln or a pair of kilns. Barley is stored in the malting, then it is soaked in water and spread on the floor to germinate. After the germination has started, the barley is heated on a grating over a smokeless fire until the germination process has been killed. The barley is then bagged up for transfer to the brewery. Plate *8* shows maltings on the Essex bank of the river Stort at Sawbridgeworth. These were built between 1850 and 1865 and were sited there because there was both canal and railway transport available. Maltings can be studied almost anywhere in Britain and a lot of work and recording needs to be done on the maltings which remain.

There are many other types of manufacturing industries, such as soap-making and chemical works, which have characteristic buildings. There are many sites and buildings which need to be recorded and studied by industrial archaeologists.

Transport

Many industrial archaeologists feel that the subject of transport is dealt with by its own band of enthusiasts. There is certainly a wealth of literature about the railways, canals and airways. This literature, however, tends to deal more with the moveable items of transport, rather than with the buildings, routes and fittings of the services. It is in these areas of study that the industrial archaeologist can find scope for his enthusiasm and carry out valuable recording work.

Until the introduction of motorways in Britain in the late 1950s, the road pattern had evolved on top of itself. The main road arteries of the country had, in essence, been laid down by the Romans and this pattern had been kept. The medieval traveller had followed the Roman road because it was the only trackway available to him. When the turnpike roads were made they were usually improvements to the existing road pattern and not new routes. The turnpike road became the surfaced road required by the motor car and the alignment remained more or less the same. Only at the beginning of the 1930s were new roads cut in virgin country. The East Lancashire road, which was opened in the mid-1930s, with the Mersey Tunnel connecting it through to the Wirral peninsula, is typical of this new construction. The Kingston By-pass and the North Circular road are similar roads dating from the 1930s. It was only the explosive growth of the motor car and

9   The toll house on A4, Thatcham, Berkshire

motor transport which caused the road pattern to be re-thought in the 1950s and the motorway system came into being.

The industrial archaeologist interested in the road pattern of this country has a great deal to investigate and record dating from the beginning of the Industrial Revolution to the present day. Whilst the original structure of the early turnpike roads has been overlaid many times, it is often visible again when cable trenches are opened up or when new road works leave the old road to one side. The turnpike trusts set up toll houses, milestones, boundary posts and pumps along their roads and these remain to be recorded. Plate 9 shows the toll house at Thatcham in Berkshire which has now been demolished. An even more exciting example existed at Halfway, between Newbury and Hungerford, and looked like a china Staffordshire cottage!

Roads had to cross rivers and the bridges carrying them are an important element of the history of civil engineering. There are many fine stone bridges such as the English bridge at Shrewsbury, Telford's bridge at Over in Gloucester, or the Skerton bridge at Lancaster. Iron was introduced into bridge building by Abraham Darby at Ironbridge in Shropshire. This had many successors: the Chepstow road bridge, Coalport bridge, and Lary bridge at Plymouth. Cast iron was quickly replaced by wrought iron and it is in this material that the great British road bridges were built. The Menai suspension bridge and the lesser Conway suspension bridge by Telford and the Clifton suspension bridge by Brunel are examples of this period. Plate *10* shows Telford's suspension bridge at Conway, built in 1826, and Robert Stephenson's tubular railway bridge beside it, built in 1848. The same group of bridges contains the Union bridge over the Tweed, Marlow bridge over the Thames and Hammersmith bridge. Great present-day suspension bridges carry British roads over the Firth of Forth and the Severn and have been developed for use all over the world.

The development of the motor car brought about a new series of road-side features which should be studied by the industrial archaeologist. Road signs were erected, firstly by the motoring organizations and then by the county authorities. These have now all been changed to match the continental system and very few remain in place. Soon no one will remember what a 'Major Road Ahead' sign looked like! Petrol was supplied in cans of two-gallon capacity before the advent of the petrol pump. Petrol pumps have changed in design over the years of this century. A hand-operated pump must be a rarity and few of the early electric pumps are still at work. The garages which lined our roads in the 1930s have mostly been replaced

10   The tubular bridge built by Robert Stephenson and the suspension bridge built by Thomas Telford at Conway

as it is part of the oil companies' policy always to be up to date. There is an excellent garage of the 1920s period behind the sea front at Paignton. Small garages can be found in remote areas, which, because they are not tied to one of the large companies, still retain a 1930s form. Transport cafes are also part of the 1930s roadside scene. There is a cafe at Aldermaston on the A4 with a central tower and an identical one on the A30 outside Basingstoke. All these should be recorded before they are demolished. Current speeds make them unnecessary for either car or lorry drivers.

The canal system of this country was one of the factors behind the technological explosion which is called the Industrial Revolution. Coal could be transported easily all over Britain when the canal network was brought into being. The industrial archaeologist should look for the monuments associated with the running of the canals and with the social life on the canals. There are many monuments such as the Dundas and Avoncliffe aqueducts on the Kennet and Avon Canal which are well known but it is the lesser equipment, such as the Acraman's crane at the Dundas basin where the Somerset Coal Canal joined the Kennet and Avon, the wharves at Pewsey, Burbage, and Honey Street on the same canal which need to be recorded. In 1963 the volunteer lengthsmen inspected the whole of the Kennet and Avon Canal and identified 360 objects, such as milestones, culverts and cottages which were associated with the canal. Whilst these are known, they were not recorded in any detail at the time. This indicates the scale of the fieldwork still required to record the canals of Britain.

Plate *11* shows the round house at Marston Meysey in Wiltshire on the Thames and Severn Canal. This round house served as a lengthsman's and lock keeper's cottage. As a family house it must have resembled the nest of the long-tailed tit! The ground floor at canal level was a wash house and tool shed and this was not connected to the upper floors. The living room was on the first floor, accessible from an overbridge; the only bedroom was on the second floor. The roof is an upturned cone with a central hopper-head and rainwater pipe and this caused the roof timbers to decay. These round houses have become derelict because they were badly designed. As well as the obvious monuments associated with the canals there are others with less obvious connections. The brickworks at Great Linford in Buckinghamshire were brought into being to provide bricks for the Grand Junction Canal and they continued to send bricks out along the canal for other uses after its completion.

There are many lengths of canal which were never completed and these are marked by disconnected stretches, incomplete lock chambers and embankments that are meaningless. Other canals (the North Walsham and Dilham Canal in Norfolk is an example) have been derelict for so long that

11   The round house at Marston Meysey, Wiltshire

the route and works have been almost completely obliterated. The industrial monument which was never completed and the monument which has been obliterated are just as worthy of study as those which still exist in a complete form. The fieldworker has just as much a duty to study these as he has to record buildings or objects which are so complete that reading them is easy and full photography is possible.

Railways are at present undergoing considerable change. Electrification is spreading its tentacles right up into Scotland, stations are being modernized and reduced to more economic units and lines are still being closed. All this brings great pressure on the industrial archaeologist.

The fieldworker who interests himself in the early forms of the railway system has to start well back in the eighteenth century when parts of this country were being interlaced with plateways. The early industrialists laid railways, which were made of flat cast-iron plates with an inside upstanding lip, to transport their wagons carrying coal, ore or stone. Indeed, some examples exist where the 'rails' were, in fact, baulks of timber with a flat strap of wrought iron on the inside edge. One of the author's great thrills as an industrial archaeologist occurred when he found that a copper-mine railway in the Tilberthwaite Fells had been one of these wooden railways. Northumberland is criss-crossed by plateways which now exist as cart roads, or cycle tracks used by miners on their way to and from the pits. The plumbago mine in Borrowdale had a plateway underground, which was installed in 1798. Pieces of that plate were exposed when the flash floods of 1966 gouged great chasms in the waste tip. Bertram Baxter's book, *Stone Blocks and Iron Rails*, is a history of plateways but it covers only a small proportion of all the plateways which once existed.

Industrial archaeologists should concern themselves with the various stages in the development of the railway station. No study has been made, for instance, of the different schemes for standardization and prefabrication which were put forward by Brunel, Brassey and others. Goods yards and their buildings and equipment have also not been studied. The London coal yards have nearly all been sold for housing or buried under modern distribution arrangements. In these yards the railway trucks moved along parallel tracks and were taken to the individual coal dealer's stock piles on tracks which ran at right angles. The connections were made by hydraulically powered truck turntables. Coal yards also have little sheds where the individual dealers set up their offices. These in themselves have characteristic designs.

There is a wealth of study to be done on the ancillary equipment of the railways. The signal poles with their local variations ought to be recorded before they are all removed to be replaced by electric-light signalling with very long-range control. The detailed study of signal boxes should be carried out before these are all replaced by long-range signal boxes. The various types of mileposts, ownership boundary markers and the like should all be sought out and recorded.

Railways have many great civil-engineering works which have been well documented. Bridges such as the tubular bridge at Conway (Plate 10), the High Level bridge at Newcastle and the great bridge over the Tamar at Saltash are examples of these. However, there are many other structures which are not nearly so well known. Until the publication of *The Girder Bridge* by P. S. A. Berridge the arch bridge with a triangular-sectioned bow built by Brunel over the Thames at Windsor was more or less unknown. Now its place in the bridge-design sequence is established. The minor brick bridges at Maidenhead and Gatehampton, where the main line to Bristol crosses the Thames, are structures to be classed with the Wharnecliffe viaduct at Hanwell or the Digswell viaduct just to the north of Welwyn Garden City. Tunnels and embankments, although not so visually dramatic as bridges, are equally important. Many of them go back to the time when the plateways were first constructed.

Airports have grown up since the beginning of this century and there are remains of the air-transport industry up and down the country. The lighter-than-air machine did not have an airfield in the conventional sense but a large shed and a mooring post were necessary for an airship. The sheds at Cardington in Bedfordshire have been protected as historic monuments although their actual working life was so short. The airship R101 was erected there and was housed in one of the sheds. R100 was delivered to be stabled there after its erection at Howden in Yorkshire. R101 was lost at Louvain in Belgium on her maiden voyage and this effectively killed the development of the airship. The aircraft of the 'wire and canvas' period did have substantial buildings and small airfields. Several of these exist in an unaltered form; the airfield just south of Ryde in the Isle of Wight still has its airport buildings. Long-distance air traffic has moved away from its original airports because these have become surrounded by suburban housing which has prevented the lengthening of runways. Croydon airport, which was the main airport for London before the 1939–45 war, has now been absorbed into a local authority housing estate but its control tower of 1928 still retains its original mass and form. Wartime aerodromes still exist from the 1939–45 period and one often comes across control towers, hangars and runways in the middle of the English countryside. Modern airports need not yet concern the industrial archaeologist. However, as with Croydon and Hendon, the time may come when Heathrow and Gatwick airports could conceiveably be redundant and if it does, the industrial archaeologist will be involved in a huge area of fieldwork.

Building materials

The sites where building materials were produced are numerous and range from stone quarries and brickworks to factories where industrialized units are made.

Stone quarries exist in many parts of Britain but the most important are those which lie on the limestone beds. This geological range starts on the Portland peninsula and finishes in Yorkshire but also covers the great stone areas around Bath, the Cotswolds, and Ketton and Clipsham on the Northampton–Rutland border. Many of the quarries are no longer working and contain much to interest the industrial archaeologist. The basic form of the quarry is important and so are the cranes which hoisted out the stone and the saws with which it was cut. Portland is still active and the stone trade has a small museum there. Underground quarries exist at Box, near Bath, where the stone is cut out of the ground by sawing. The stone then weathers and hardens to the honey colour which was so popular in Bath and in other towns to which it could be transported. Roofing stone was mined at Stonesfield in Oxfordshire and in Collyweston in Northampton-shire. Here the quarrymen worked in the summer underground and brought the stone slates up to be frosted in stacks in the nearby fields during the winter.

Slate is quarried in the Lake District, in Wales and in Cornwall. Although slate is now less used than formerly as a roofing material, the quarries are still open to produce large sheets of sawn or riven slate for the facing of buildings. Some slate was mined in open quarries such as the deep pit at Delabole in Cornwall, or Llanberis and Blaenau Festiniog in Wales, or in mines such as the huge one in Coniston Old Man in north Lancashire. These quarries are full of interest. In some areas there are quarries still with their railways in place, with the engine houses on the inclined planes and with compressor houses for the pneumatic tools. There is a fine pelton wheel serving the compressors in the Coniston quarry. This was served by a water pipe with a 150m (500-ft) head from Low Water. These areas are so remote that the scrap dealer cannot make the collection of scrap worthwhile.

Brickworks are one of the commonest industrial monuments in this country. However, they have been severely reduced in number and this is one area of work for which the industrial archaeologist is urgently required. The Reading beds of brick earth were very active in the last century and in the early part of this century but by 1973 there were only two brickworks still at work in Berkshire. The biggest brickworks are those surviving on the Oxford clays which stretch from east of Peterborough through Bed-fordshire and Buckinghamshire to Oxford. Here the clay has to be pressed into shape, for only with pressure is the clay given cohesion. The bricks of the Oxford clays contain $2\frac{1}{2}$ per cent of mineral oil, which assists the firing process. The kilns in use at brickworks on the Oxford clays are always the very large Hoffmann or Belgian kilns in which the long rectangles contain numerous cells, each with its own door. There the bricks are fired and each cell is active in successive stages of a consecutive process. Coal is inserted through holes in the roof of the kiln onto the bricks. The kilns never go out and the bricks take about seven days to go through all the stages of the process in the kiln.

Bricks are labour intensive in their manufacture and their use in building is even more so. In the late 1950s industrialized building came to this country from Europe. This implies a different and expensive type of factory for the construction of the concrete panels which replace the

12   The batching plant at a pre-cast concrete factory, Rushden, Northamptonshire

conventional brickwork. Economic considerations have closed down several of these pre-cast concrete producing factories. The factories consist basically of a large shed, with internal cranes running the whole length of the roof. On the floor there are several steel forms on which the panels are cast and the concrete is delivered by overhead transport from a central batching and mixing plant. Plate *12* shows part of a pre-cast concrete producing factory at Rushden in Northamptonshire. This was built in 1968 and in 1973 it was gutted and sold to a caravan-making company.

Concrete requires cement, gravel and sand in its manufacture. Gravel and sand are obtained from pits in the river valleys and these are dominated by the grading plants. The grading takes place in asbestos or corrugated-iron sheds where the material is first stored in hoppers before being sorted in rotating screens which separate the various grades into further hoppers where they are stored until collected for distribution to the various yards or builders. These grading units have a sculptural quality which makes them quite exciting to the industrial archaeologist. Cement is produced in large factories situated on the chalk or limestone beds. The first kilns were built in Kent on the North Downs. Large modern cement factories can be seen at Northfleet, Rugby and Tring.

Timber has been produced in Britain for a very long time, but most of the timber used in the present-day building industry is imported from Scandinavia or Canada. Originally, timber was processed in the yards where it was to be used. The logs were sawn into planks with pit saws and one man would be in the pit getting covered with sawdust while the other man was on top of the log. This is graphically described in George Sturt's book, *The Wheelwright's Shop*. Some estates had permanently built saw mills and there are good examples of these at Tyninghame in East Lothian and at Gunton Park in Norfolk. That at Gunton Park was clearly built as a temporary mill in the late eighteenth century. Its wooden walls were not triangulated and so it has twisted a bit out of shape. However, two water-wheels drove a conventional circular saw and a reciprocating saw, and power was also taken off for a small corn mill in the roof.

Agricultural industry

Some industrial archaeologists would claim that there is no scope for them in the field of agriculture. If one thinks of the pure process of farming that is no doubt the case. For the interested fieldworker the following points may be of some value, and he may find scope in studying these items.

Farm buildings themselves are basically the responsibility of the student of vernacular architecture. However, in the nineteenth century, model farms run on industrial principles were set up. Publications such as J. C. Loudon's *Encyclopedia of Agriculture* led the way to the planned farmyard with 'flow line' techniques for the distribution of fodder and the storage of the produce. The author was excited by his examination of the Home Farm on the National Trust's estate at Coleshill in Berkshire. Here the slope of the site was used to advantage when the agent to the estate, E. Moore, laid out the farmery for the Earl of Radford in 1862. At the top of the yard the barns received the hay, corn and straw for storage, use or despatch. The central feature, surmounted by a bell-cote and chimney, was the granary and engine house. In the granary, line shafting from the steam engine drove thrashing machines, winnowing machines, grinding, bruising and cake-crushing machines. From this central point a narrow-gauge rail track ran down through the central wing of stock houses and piggeries to the bottom wing which contained the cattle houses. Trucks were pushed along the track or were towed by horses. At the junctions of the track, where the wings of the buildings crossed at right angles, there were small turntables. The natural slope of the hill made it easier to swill out the manure in the stock houses so that it was collected in tanks below the farm. Similar farms were built by the Prince Consort at Windsor and the Duke of Bedford at Woburn. Northumberland contains quite a lot of this type of farm where the land owners, who were also coal owners, built large farms which had steam engines and horse engines to power the machinery. These farms, too, had their own ranges of farmhouses and tied cottages for the farm workers.

The actual buildings may not create much interest, but the industrial archaeologist should be on the lookout for new types of construction. The mass-concrete barn, built in 1869, at Buscot in north-west Berkshire, may well have been the first agricultural building in which Portland cement was used as a matrix for concrete. This barn is 49m (162 ft) long, 20m (65 ft) wide, 14m (45 ft) high at the ridge and 3·80m (12 ft 6 in.) high at the eaves. In its way it matches the Great Coxwell tithe barn, which was built in the thirteenth century only a few miles away. Buscot was built up as an industrialized agricultural estate in the 1860s and 1870s. There was a narrow-gauge railway with three locomotives which ran round the farms joining the brick yard, the gravel pit, the various farm buildings and the sugar-beet-into-alcohol refinery which was situated on an island in the Thames by Buscot lock.

Farms had many sources of power for their machinery. The horse wheel house is mentioned earlier in this chapter. The use of permanently mounted steam engines was known on the larger farms, such as those in Northumberland and at Coleshill, but it was more usual to use a portable steam engine which could be brought up to the barn to drive machinery as necessary and the steam engine and its driver were often hired from a contractor. Waterwheels which drove farm machinery still exist and a lot of fieldwork needs to be done on these as they are not shown on the smaller scale Ordnance Survey maps and have been overlooked in consequence. The farm buildings designed by J. C. Loudon for two farms on Matthew Boulton's Great Tew estate both contained waterwheels, situated below ground, which drove machinery in the barns above. A waterwheel drove the fodder-producing machines for the horses required to serve the ore port of Morwellham on the Tamar. This stands in the farm a little way behind the workers' houses which backed the main port basin. In Dorset, Rex Wailes found many waterwheels for farm use. These, and the drawing of the waterwheel at Forston in the Cerne valley, are detailed in his Newcomen Society paper, *Dorset Watermills,* in vol. 35 of the Transactions, 1962–3. The Forston wheel was built by Lott and Walne in 1910 and drove the thrashing machine and vacuum-milking machine in the adjacent byre.

Many industrial processes are associated with farm products and have buildings worthy of study. In dairy country, many railway sidings have milk-processing plant, where milk was collected and put into rail tankers to be sent to the large towns. Now many of these are no longer served by railways and the tankers are carried by road as this gives a quicker service to the bottling plant and dairy buildings in the towns. At the end of the 1930s cold-storage plants were built on railway sidings. These were served on one side by the sidings and on the other by road-transport vehicles. Whilst these were essentially a wartime requirement, they have been superseded by later processing methods and are frequently in use by other traders.

Grain silos were once a feature of the railway scene but, although still in use in some cases, they are being replaced by the prefabricated type of silo —similar to those now used on farms. These concrete grain silos have a distinctive and sculptural form. Sugar-beet factories exist throughout the eastern counties of England. Here the features are very much those of any other factory. The essential components are the silo, the processing buildings and large bins for storing the unprocessed sugar beet. The agricultural industry is very much part of our country scene and much of it is worthy of record.

Housing for industrial workers

In many ways the study of housing as such is the responsibility of the architectural historian. The industrial archaeologist should not neglect the housing which has been deliberately built to serve the needs of an adjacent factory or industry. Most general books on industrial archaeology make some reference to the flax mill at Shrewsbury, built by Charles Bage in 1796, but whilst this is important because of its iron-frame construction, no one mentions the delightful curved terrace of workers' cottages which was built at the same time. This terrace forms a foil for the factory when it is viewed from the Shrewsbury side. Similar rows of workers' houses exist round the Strutt mills at Belper near Derby.

Industrial estates were built by the railway companies to house the workers in their locomotive and carriage works. The best known example of this is the housing built for Great Western workmen at Swindon, which has now been deliberately preserved. Here the rows of cottages were punctuated by larger houses for the foremen and superintendents. Similar groups of houses existed at Wolverton and Crewe, at Eastleigh and at Ashford. A delightful description of life in a railway town (Crewe) can be found in *Stokers and Pokers* by Sir Francis Head.

Benevolent factory masters with a social conscience also built estates or villages for their workers. The late eighteenth-century town of New Lanark in the Clyde valley, built by David Dale and Robert Owen, with Richard Arkwright also in association, is perhaps the best known example. Here the factories were set up and the work people were attracted to the area by the low-rental housing built by the factory masters. The Edinburgh workhouse provided many of the younger members of the work force, who were housed in their own dormitory block. The estate contained the school, institute, church and shops. Saltaire in Yorkshire, built by Sir Titus Salt, is another example. In this century, the Protestant families of the Cadburys, Rowntrees and Levers built garden cities around their factories at Bourneville, New Earswick and Port Sunlight. These were built to the new standards demonstrated at Hampstead, Welwyn and Letchworth, and had progressed from the rows of houses which had been erected at Swindon or New Lanark. The arrangement was good from the point of view of the worker but even better from the point of view of the factory masters. Better standards of health were achieved and the better conditions gave the workers a less beligerent attitude to their masters. A tied house on such an estate would be a deterrent to militancy!

As the fieldworker goes round his industrial sites he should look out for units of industrial housing. Outside the 'live' brickworks at Bletchley there is a row of houses marked 'Model Workmen's Cottages 1910 R.A.'. Elgar Road in Reading is lined on both sides with houses built by the owners of the Elgar Road brickworks. Each house is decorated with some of the terracotta samples produced at the works but they are not intended to be 'sample' houses. The demonstration of the firm's products is left to the manager's house or office block at the entrance to the brickworks. When the Oxford clays began to be exploited in Bedfordshire, the brickworks were in open country and so a garden city estate was built at Stewartby to house the families of the workers. When the housing relates to a particular industry it should be recorded and its relationship in both social and planning terms should be carefully noted.

Public services

The public services can provide the fieldworker in industrial archaeology with some of the most exciting and dramatic monuments in the discipline. Most of the present-day installations in this field have made the buildings and plant of 50 years ago redundant. The fieldworker must record these early installations before they are totally destroyed.

Electricity was first marketed on a commercial scale in London at Holborn Viaduct and in Brighton in 1882 and the first really viable power station was built at Deptford in 1889. Municipalities followed the lead given by London so that electricity was available in most towns in the country by the end of the first decade of the twentieth century. Newbury, for example, built a water-turbine generator system at Greenham Mills. A former corn mill was adapted for this purpose and later a special building was erected to the north of this to house the generator. The turbine-driven generators came first and then two gas engines were installed, at first to assist the water turbines, but later to replace them. The gas was produced from anthracite behind the generator building and the little gas holder was still there in 1968, used for oil storage. To the north of the gas engines four diesel generators were built; two at the time of the 1939–45 war and two in the late 1950s. These generator sets were very large and were beautifully maintained. As more floor space was required, the building was extended and the north end was always temporary in character.

The grid which linked the power stations on a national pattern came into being at the end of the 1930s and at that time power stations had a distinctive design. The typical large halls of brick with tall ranges of windows were surmounted by several large brick chimneys. Battersea power station is typical of this family of power stations, in which the brick generator hall is marked by chimneys at each of the four corners. The architectural embellishments of these strictly functional halls were often added by famous architects of the day: Sir Charles Reilly in the case of Lodge Road power station, Marylebone, and Sir Giles Gilbert Scott at Battersea. The power stations were coupled to large concrete cooling towers which have always had a sculptured shape brought about by the use of thin-skin concrete structures. Earlier cooling towers were made of wood, lined with wooden slats on which dripping water condensed the steam for subsequent re-use. The quality of these towers is brought out in the book by Bernard and Hilda Becher, *Anonyme Skulpturen, Eine Typologie Technischer Bauten*. The great modern power stations which have made many of the 1930s power stations redundant are built on much more functional lines. Those at Drax, Fawley and Didcot are good examples. The halls are now largely clad with lightweight materials and glass, and the chimneys have been reduced to a single multiflued stack, usually of concrete.

The design of pylons carrying the electricity cables is another study for the industrial archaeologist. There are many patterns to be seen, which have evolved over the 50 or so years of general electricity distribution. There are the common tower types standing on four legs, which curve inwards and upwards to carry the cross arms with their large ceramic insulators and cables. When cables have to cross navigable rivers the towers go up very high so that the catenary of the sagging cables still clears the masts of ships. These tall pylons can be seen at Northfleet on the Thames Estuary and at Hebburn on the river Tyne. In the centre of Wellington in Shropshire there is a very interesting electricity sub-station of distinctive 1930 style, which is surmounted by two square lattice pylons. Plate *13* shows a small cast-iron sub-station which stood on the Berkshire side of the Thames near Henley until quite recently. The decorative panels all open to reveal the switches and the incoming and outgoing cables. The firm which made these also made lamp standards, such as those of St Marylebone, and these have similar cast-iron detailing.

Gas is now made from coal in the original fashion in only a few remote gas works in the north of England and in Scotland. Gas made from coal was first made a commercial venture by the Gas Light and Coke Company when they started to supply gas in 1812. Very soon after this, other towns and cities started their own municipal gas undertakings. In Reading, the first gasworks was duplicated by the opening of a second near the mouth of the Kennet. These were in turn replaced by the third and last gasworks which was built with rail connections in the 1870s. With the Gas Act of 1927 the last carbonization plant was built on the site with the characteristic vertical retorts. Previously the retorts had been horizontal. The manufacture of gas from coal was first of all replaced by the reduction of naptha in plant which looked like a conventional oil refinery, built on earlier gasworks sites. This has very quickly been replaced by natural gas, which is pumped across Britain from the Yorkshire and Norfolk stations where the pipelines come in from the North Sea.

13 A cast iron electricity sub-station which stood on the roadside near Henley-on-Thames

Natural gas requires the retention of gas holders, which are still to be seen on the empty gasworks sites. There are some historic gas holders such as that at the Fulham gasworks which should be preserved. The large cylinders rise out of water tanks so that the cylinders expand out of each other when there is a lot of gas to store. The earlier holders supported the tanks between skeleton frameworks of steel or even cast iron. The later ones rose spirally and were self-supporting. A different type of gas holder depends on displacing the air from a rigid non-expanding tank. These were more common in Europe, as they derive from a German patent, but can be seen at Southall, Lancaster and several other British gasworks. The industrial archaeologist should attempt to record the carbonization plants before they are destroyed and should also record the various gas holders which still remain—if only for their pleasing effect.

Of all the public services, water is the one with the longest history. The importance of a steady supply of water was realized in the Elizabethan period and a waterwheel-driven pump was installed in London Bridge and served the nearby streets and houses. This proved inadequate and the important water-supply system which brought water by gravity from springs near Hertford was introduced in 1613. This was the New River. It brought water to Islington and is the basis on which the Metropolitan Water Board was founded. This live system will survive and its fieldwork is no doubt preserved in the records of the Metropolitan Water Board. However, a similar gravity system, now abandoned, is Drake's Leat, which brought water from Dartmoor to Devonport and Plymouth. Work needs to be done on this.

Steam-powered water-pumping plant is detailed earlier in this chapter. This needs to be recorded as quickly as possible before it all disappears and as much as possible should be preserved in the manner of that at Ryhope. A dramatic sphere of work waits for the industrial archaeologist in the study of reservoirs, their dams and aqueducts. The neat little dam across the Thirlmere valley in Cumbria is not on the same scale as the Boulder Dam or the dams of the Tennessee Valley Authority but it is, none the less, a good masonry dam construction. Just as important is the castellated straining well in the middle of the shoreline of Thirlmere, from which the pipeline sets out for Manchester. Along the line there are small masonry survey towers from which the tunnel line was set out and several places where the four wrought-iron pipes jump the river valleys. Similar systems exist at Haweswater, Rivington and Vrynwy where minor dams create large reservoirs to serve Manchester, Liverpool and Birmingham.

Private water supplies have largely been abandoned as houses have gone over to the public system. A lot of these abandoned systems are worthy studies for the fieldworker. For instance, in Oxfordshire there are several small waterwheels which pump by means of beams and single- or double-cylindered pumps to supply farms and field water tanks. Other water supplies were ensured by the use of a wind engine, which pumped water out of a well into a water tank at high level. Frequently a group of tied cottages can be found where a wind engine has been built on top of a water tank from which water was drawn off in the cottages by gravity.

Like everything else, the postal and telephone services are changing rapidly. The ubiquitous pillar box has been the subject of a book but the telephone kiosk has not been studied. The standard cast-iron box has a series of glass panes in each of three faces and the instrument and coin box are mounted on the fourth. This type is now being replaced by the modern four square kiosk. This has single panes of 'unbreakable' glass in each of three faces. There are odd variants to be found up and down the country. For instance, there is a single example at Roydon in Essex, where one of the kiosks produced as a result of a competition in design in 1926 has come to rest. Telephone exchanges have now come to look like any other office block. However, there are some older exchanges throughout Britain which will remain until subscriber trunk dialling makes them redundant. The 'art nouveau' telephone exchange in Reading, which has been replaced by an office-block type, is a 'listed' building. Examples like this should be sought out and recorded.

Radio and the more recent television services are products of this century. They are developing fast and the buildings which house them are straightforward ones with ranges of office units and the stages and studios behind them. The transmission masts of the original early radio service were placed in groups and these have now been replaced by single tall masts. Television is transmitted from similar high masts, or from parabolic reflector to parabolic receiver mounted on sturdy towers on high ridges or in the centres of cities on tall towers. The Post Office tower in London's West End and the tower at Stokenchurch on the Chiltern ridge are examples. Perhaps it is too early to regard the radio and television industry as worthy of fieldwork but this does not mean that the artefacts of the industry—early microphones and radio and television receivers—should not be collected and preserved.

The industry of recreation

The seaside and other holiday areas are full of industrial remains which are fun for the industrial archaeologist to study. The pier and pier railway date from the early days of the nineteenth century. When the people who had travelled by coach to Brighton in the wake of the Prince Regent were tired of the social round of the promenade and the Pavilion gardens, they turned towards the sea for their entertainment. Sea air was a valuable restorative in the eyes of the 'Spa' doctors and was best breathed some distance out from the shore. The promenade was therefore extended seawards as a pier. It was also fashionable to travel to a resort by boat and the pier was where one disembarked. This was particularly true of the piers on the Thames Estuary, such as at Southend, or the piers of the Severn Estuary, such as at Weston-super-Mare, Clevedon or Ilfracombe. Piers in the estuaries had to be very long to enable boats to tie up at all stages of the tide and so, to make things easier, a pier railway was built to connect the seaward end with the landward end. These piers are expensive to maintain and they are being destroyed in the minor resorts because of lack of financial support. When they carry small theatres or dance halls there is a better financial return but with our short holiday season even that is doubtful.

Behind the sea front in some of the larger resorts there is the fun fair. Study of these is required because they no longer have such an appeal to the travelling public and may therefore not survive for much longer. The permanent fun fairs, such as the Battersea Fun Fair and the Spanish City at Whitley Bay, contain some interesting mechanical fun-making contrivances, although much of their works are hidden behind the lath-and-plaster, stage-set type of architecture which these fun fairs seem to enjoy. The Scenic Railway, the Tunnel of Love (or Horrors!), and the Big Wheel are all worthy of detailed study. One wonders if the great Ferris Wheel at Blackpool, which had a very short life, was ever properly recorded. Frith and Co., and other postcard makers, photographed it in a scenic sense but was its mechanism ever carefully studied? The Prater Wheel in Vienna was a larger Ferris wheel than the one at Blackpool and is to be preserved by the city authorities.

The pleasure gardens of Vauxhall and Ranelagh contained entertainment booths in the eighteenth century and it is a short step from these to the Victorian music hall. This element of entertainment has been reproduced on television but do we really know what the music hall was like at the end of the nineteenth century? The early cinema grew up in the music hall as a 'turn' but quickly grew away from it into buildings of its own. Relatively little is known about the early cinema buildings, as the industry rapidly outgrew them. With the coming of sound in the early 1930s a new and more opulent cinema form came into being. Whilst these cinemas had some suggestion of the impermanence of the fairground, their opulence, whether Moorish or baroque or plain jazzy modern, was there to advertise and to draw the patrons in. The New Victoria cinema and the Granada at Tooting are examples of the above and are to be preserved. The 1930s were the days of the 2,000-seat cinema but now the tendency is towards the intimate cinema, no longer rising tier on tier but with a simple ramped floor and perhaps no more than 600 seats.

Supplying the cinema industry there were large groups of buildings in which films were made. In the early days these required large areas of north-facing glazing. The studio of Heinrich Herkommer at Bushey is typical of this period and still exists in the form in which it was built. Lighting techniques improved and the sets were built in 'stages' where all the lighting was artificial and all the sets were false. This produced studios like those at Denham in Buckinghamshire or at Elstree. Here the stages were built in ranges behind the dressing rooms, processing laboratories and office blocks.

Perhaps the buildings associated with the theatre and the cinema fall more properly into the brief of the art and architectural historian but the early production units of the film industry do not. For the industrial archaeologist the field of the entertainment industry offers great scope.

The foregoing sections of this chapter give the industrial archaeologist some idea of the scope which exists for his activities in the field. The list is by no means complete, indeed it would be folly to attempt to make it so. As the industrial archaeologist gets into the spirit of the discipline and gains experience, he will see, on the one hand, where his interests lie and, on the other, what the pressures and priorities are for the use of his experience. He will begin to work on one facet of his chosen subject only to realize that he must step aside to record other items which are interrelated. In order to complete a unit of work he may need to be strong willed in order to avoid being taken down an irrelevant by-way.

Often, too, there are rewarding moments for the industrial archaeologist in the field. He may make a discovery of some object which no one else has found, or which had not been thought to exist. The cupola furnace at the foundry at Bucklebury described in Chapter 9 is such a find. After finding it, the author did not realize its significance until a fellow industrial archaeologist found its true description, 'stave cupola' in a mid-nineteenth-century textbook where it was disparagingly described as 'the old type of furnace'. It is not known if another furnace of this type exists in Britain. Plate *14* shows a horizontal windmill mounted at low level on a wind-engine tower in a nursery garden at Potter Heigham in Norfolk. These machines are held in the same veneration as perpetual motion machines and yet here is one which cannot be very old, properly thought out and connected to a water pump. This needs to be carefully written up with a note about its designer if possible, the reason for abandoning the wind engine—and so on. Plate *15*

14   A horizontal windmill mounted on a wind engine tower at Potter
Heigham, Norfolk

15　The coaling staithes and a steam crane, Amble, Northumberland

shows the coaling staithes at Amble in Northumberland and also an
associated steam crane. This is part of the equipment no longer in use of the
Northumberland coalfield. It is a big proposition to deal with properly as a
field object and yet it needs this sort of treatment. It would be wrong if
destruction of monuments such as this went on without any records being
made. It is the industrial archaeologist who must absorb the discipline and
step into the breach to do the fieldwork.

2. The various types of fieldwork

The industrial archaeologist may be called upon to take part in various types of fieldwork. Whilst he may be pursuing a certain aspect of the subject as a hobby—and therefore at his own pace—he may be asked to do other types of fieldwork because of the pressures of re-development or the threat of destruction of an industrial site. Many industrial archaeologists are known for their work in a particular subject but they frequently get asked to assist with work on some other industry. The author has, therefore, set down criteria for working in three categories: the survey of an industry in a given area; the survey in depth of a single industrial unit; and the survey of an area or unit in an emergency. Clearly these categories overlap but it is hoped that these criteria will help the industrial archaeologist to carry out his fieldwork so that he can achieve the maximum result in what is, inevitably, restricted time.

The survey of an industry in a given area

Most industrial archaeologists start out on their own or with a team in some form of industrial survey over a given area. Local industrial archaeology groups set themselves the target of studying the various monuments in their area, often by doing a given industrial subject each year. The Southampton University Industrial Archaeology Group have, for example, studied the milling systems of Hampshire. The results of this study were published in vol. xxv of *The Proceedings of the Hampshire Field Club*, under the title 'A Gazetteer of the Water, Wind and Tide Mills of Hampshire'. Eighteen members of the group took part in the survey, and were joined by a further nine from outlying groups. Of course it is not necessary for the work to be done by a large group. The author carried out the fieldwork for *The Mills of the Isle of Wight* accompanied only by his wife. Similarly he has done surveys of the milling systems of Berkshire, Bedfordshire and Wiltshire and, with Eric Griffith, has covered the mills of Northumberland.

The industrial archaeologist setting out to do an area survey must start by locating in advance all the likely sites for his chosen industry in that area.

A day spent in examining the 6-in. maps of about 1900 will save a great deal of time in the field. As the 6-in. maps of that period do not have grid references, the industrial archaeologist will have to note down the sites which he has to examine in relation to some known landmark—'one mile north-west of parish church', for example. The date of the maps will also be important because by choosing a certain date, usually about 1900, the live sites will be noted together with the disused sites. Armed with the list of possible sites and the 1-in. or 2½-in. maps, the industrial archaeologist can commence his fieldwork. Some industrial processes have natural boundaries and some have geological boundaries, whilst others relate to the watershed. The fieldworkers may be working in an area which is at variance with this as he will probably be working to a county administrative unit. He should therefore be prepared to carry his investigations into adjoining areas, although he may not need to publish the results of that part of his fieldwork which lies outside the given area. For example, a person working on the brickworks of Bedfordshire must, of necessity, extend his survey to Oxford on one side and to Whittlesey in Cambridgeshire on the other, as these sites all belong to the same geological formation known as the Oxford Clays.

The purpose of an area survey is to list all the sites associated with the chosen industry in that area. It is therefore just as important to know the sites on which there are now no remains as it is to know those on which the industrial unit is complete. The completed survey will be used by all manner of people in quite different ways. Local authorities may wish to consult the survey in order to determine whether there is any example of the industrial unit which needs the protection of the Planning Acts and it is therefore necessary for the industry to be seen as a whole in the area. Technical colleges or universities may be studying the economics or the geography of the industry and an area survey, if available, would amplify their work.

To what depth, therefore, should the industrial archaeologist go when he is doing fieldwork over an area in this way? In the first place he should visit every known site, as well as those sites on which the industry may have been carried on but about which there is no documentary evidence. At each site he should investigate the extent of the remains and, if there has been total destruction of buildings and plant, he should look for evidence of the trade and how it was powered. Sites where the buildings remain, possibly derelict, should be recorded in greater detail; the shape and size of the buildings and the road or rail layout to the site should be noted. However, when it comes to existing, possibly working, units of the industry, these should be recorded in considerable detail. At this stage the fieldworker should content himself with fairly general photographs of the site, with relevant overall measurements and with details of the machinery or other equipment. If the industry is well established and still at work, the industrial archaeologist should photograph work in process, the tools used, the product and the men, as well as the surroundings in which they are working.

This may seem a large specification for a survey but it should be borne in mind that most of the areas of industry which are the subject of such a survey are already seriously reduced and threatened by changing methods and later developments. In terms of time, therefore, it is not likely that much will remain that will occupy the fieldworker for long. Where he does need to spend time will be in those units which are fully equipped and it is in these areas that his fieldwork is most useful. For instance, in the case of mills it is important to investigate the water-supply arrangements of the various sites but it is much more important to record the gearing and the arrangement of millwork in those units where it exists complete. In the county of Berkshire there are some 112 mill sites but of these, in 1963, there were only 12 mills with complete sets of gearing, although this was not always in good condition. This pattern is generally repeated throughout Britain. Thus the time-consuming process of full recording is restricted to a relatively small number of units. Other industries have almost similar patterns.

As the work progresses, the records for the area survey will have been assembled in the fieldworker's own private collection. He will then need to prepare this material for some form of distribution or publication. In the first instance it is usual to prepare a basic list of all the examples found. This can be done as a series of short, snappy paragraphs—not necessarily in telegraphic English—which give the name of the site, its National Grid reference number and a brief description of the remains. This must always be coupled to a map which sets out the distribution of the sites so that the pattern of the industry in the area can be readily seen. The pamphlet *Gazetteer of Mills in Hampshire* carries notes such as the following which show the standard for which to aim when publishing a first list of sites:

HUNTON, R. TEST   168 483 397

Mill demolished early this century. No remains except a five-foot fall of water and a wheel pit.

SHERFIELD ON LODDON   169 683 582

Longbridge Mill. Half timbered at one end, brick and weatherboard, tiled roof. Cast iron undershot wheel. Most machinery present. Separate mill house. Mill in use powered by electricity.

Fred Roberts of Newbury in his paper 'A Brief Survey of Brickwork Sites in West Berkshire' published in *Bulletin of Industrial Archaeology in C.B.A. Group 9, No. 16,* lists 20 sites. Thirteen of these brickwork sites had absolutely no remains at all, and the knowledge of what the sites really contained had to be gained from maps as the kilns usually had distinctive shapes. The seven sites on which remains can be identified have been examined in some depth, and three sites which have an almost complete layout of buildings have been described in some detail.

If the industrial archaeologist is relatively unskilled in fieldwork but can use his camera and a notebook, then he will find the area survey of an industry very rewarding. At first he will be finding sites and not necessarily reading them with intelligence. As he gets further into his subject and meets other industrial archaeologists he will gain more skill in the identification of sites. Later still he will be able to interpret his finds with certainty. This may mean that some sites have to be re-examined, but the fieldworker will none the less produce a valid document. His primary tools are his eyes, his feet, his notebook and, lastly, his camera.

The survey in depth of a single industrial unit

The fieldworker may wish to devote a considerable amount of attention to recording and investigating a single industrial unit. The reason for wanting to do this may be that the industrial unit was found to be so important during an area survey, or because the unit is the only example of the industry in a particular area. The value of the study in depth is that the fieldwork can be combined with research into archives so that a full description of the site and its history can be published.

How should the fieldworker set about his survey of an industrial unit? Before actually getting out his tools and his camera he should walk around the site and its buildings to see the extent of recording required and to get some idea of the order in which he should carry out the survey. The next stage should be to take exterior photographs of important buildings and to take comprehensive photographs which show the site and the relationship between one part and another. Having completed the exterior survey the fieldworker should proceed to photograph the interiors of the buildings and the relevant machinery or equipment in relation to these interiors. If it is no longer working, the unit should be examined to find the 'flow lines' from the entry of material to the despatch of the finished product but, if it is still at work, the study of the unit will be much more rewarding and at the same time the fieldworker will understand more about its industrial use. If the products of the industry remain in a warehouse these should be examined. After the various photographs have been taken, the important buildings should be measured and their construction noted. The machines should be measured and the different means of transmitting power should be recorded. After the site has been completely recorded, the fieldworker will probably wish to couple his findings to background research. The minimum amount of research would give the names of the owners and the valuation of the buildings. Frequently letters, books and catalogues of the complex will exist in the office and these should be examined to determine the level of industry and the variations in the products over the years.

To give the reader an idea of the depth of fieldwork required, the author describes, in the following pages, his examination of Grovelands Brick-works in Reading. The firm, S. & E. Collier, closed the works in April 1967 as it was no longer profitable to continue to make bricks by hand and to occupy such a valuable site in a residential area of Reading. The works were auctioned shortly afterwards and bought as housing land. Because of difficulties in getting planning permission, the demolition of the site was delayed for about a year. The author carried out his work in July and August 1967 and this occupied several weekends and some days of holidays.

The site of the Grovelands Brickworks covered some 40 acres. On the west the site is bounded by Water Road but the remaining sides had been dug away by the clay working until the boundary of the site had been reached. The main clay pits were about a mile away and the clay was transported on a cable railway back to the works over woods and fields which have now been built over. The layout of the site was complicated and the author was fortunate to obtain an insurance plan of the site before fieldwork was begun. Figure *1* is a copy of this plan and from it the reader will see that there are various elements of this factory which do not depend on each other but which are complete units in themselves. The products of the factory were bricks, tiles, terracotta, pottery, and cement tiles and the descriptions which follow are dealt with in this same order.

Plate *16* is the south-east view of the complex taken from the boundary fence. The trees on the right hand side of the plate mark the clay face on the boundary. The foreground is the site of the terracotta warehouse which had been abandoned some time before the closure of the works. The build-ing on the right (*A* on plan) is the one which housed the Hoffmann or Belgian kiln with its chimney to the left. The range of buildings on the left is the tile factory, *C*, with lift housings on the roof and its chimney on its right. The semi-demolished engine house, *H*, is in the distance behind the two chimneys.

The author started his recording in the brick-making unit, *B*. At the north end of this building the clay was extruded and prepared before being

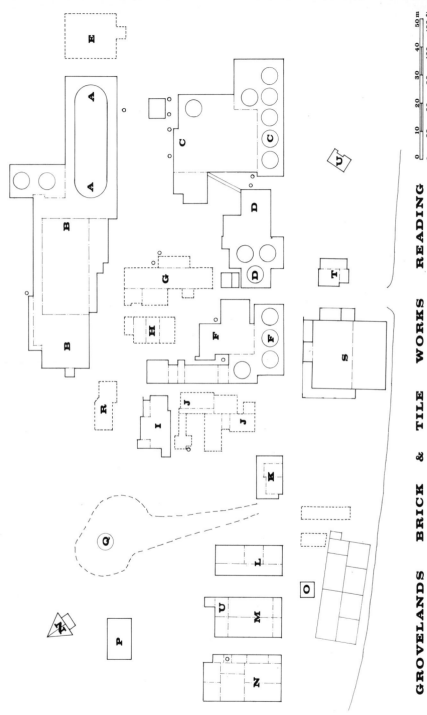

1   Plan of Grovelands Brick and Tile Works, Reading

Figure 1 **Plan of Grovelands Brick and Tile Works, Reading.**

A No 5 kiln house with Hoffmann kiln
B No 5 factory for hand-made bricks
C No 4 factory for tile making
D No 3 factory for tile making
E Terracotta warehouse (demolished)
F No 2 factory. The pottery with the crushing mill, pug mill and carpenter's shop
G No 6 factory (demolished)
H Coal store, gas plant and engine house (demolished)
I Engineering shop
J Muffle kiln, engine house, machine house
K Garages

L Tractors and garage
M Stables, cottage and cement tile factory
N No 7 factory with boilers etc.
O Garage and sample house, formerly ambulance and fire station
P Sand store
Q Wash mill
R Fitter's store
S Warehouses No 1 and No 2
T Office block
U Cottage

The large circles show downdraught kilns, the small circles are chimneys.

taken up to the brick-makers on each of the four floors above the tunnel dryers at ground level. He photographed the pug mills and tunnel dryers and then photographed the brick-maker's stool or bench (Plate *17*) and the various moulds and tools. At the end of the tunnel dryers at ground-floor level there was a traverser which carried the trucks from any one of the exits of the tunnel dryer to the track which ran down either side of the Hoffmann kiln. The inside of the Hoffmann kiln was empty and so the interior was photographed (Plate *18*). The upper level of the kiln was the level at which the coal was poured through the small holes onto the bricks during the firing process. The hot air above the kiln was used for further drying of the 'green' bricks. The air was drawn down through ducts in the floor to the central collecting flue and then to the main chimney. To the north of the Hoffmann kiln there were two downdraught kilns where the specially shaped bricks were fired.

The building *C* was the factory where roofing tiles, both plain and pan tiles, were made. Factory *D* to the north-west of *C* was built in 1938 as an extension of *C*. The two buildings contained ten downdraught kilns where the tiles were burnt after they had been dried on the upper levels of the buildings. The clay was received in the machine house at the north-east corner of building *C*. Here it passed through the pug mills and was carried in the lifts to the various tile-maker's benches at each window opening on the upper floors. After moulding, the tiles were stored on the hack racks to

16   The south-east view of Grovelands Brick and Tile Works, Reading

17   A brick maker's stool or bench in the hand-made brick factory at Grovelands

18   The interior of the Hoffmann kiln at Grovelands

19   A crowding barrow at Grovelands

get the superficial drying completed before they were loaded into the down-draught kilns. After burning, tiles were carried in a crowding barrow (Plate *19*). This is a typical brick-maker's barrow; the wheel has a bifurcated spoke and is mounted so that the barrow, when loaded correctly, has a centre of gravity almost directly over the wheel.

The next building to be investigated was the pottery, building *F* on the plan, and here all forms of domestic earthenware were made. Even at the end of the factory's life this pottery was turning out egg crocks, mixing bowls, jugs and flower pots. At the beginning of the century it was producing a glazed pottery, in blue or green, known as 'Silchester Ware'. A lot of this was based on Roman pottery from nearby Silchester or from medieval designs. The potters' wheels were all in place and on the racks behind the wheels were several examples of 'green' pots drying out but unfired. This factory (Plate *20*) contained four downdraught kilns. The buildings around the pottery and in the centre of the whole site contained the engineers' workshops, the joiners' shops, the pattern-makers' shop and the mould stores (Plate *21*).

The range of buildings to the north of the complex of engineering shops had already been lent to a firm of builder's plant hirers and so the interiors had been gutted and were not available for inspection by the author. He

20 The pottery and the engineer's shops at Grovelands

21   The interior of the mould store at Grovelands

photographed the exteriors of the buildings, N, to complete the record. However, as the machinery had been taken out, he could not determine the processes used in making the cement tiles which were the designated product of this range. Standing to one side of the site near the road there was the ambulance and fire station. This, like the office block, T, was built as a sample house. The old wash mill, Q, where the clay was reduced to a slurry and where the pebbles and fossils were removed, was overgrown and filled with bullrushes. This, and the corrugated-iron sand store, P, stood in the old clay pit.

The last items to be recorded were the warehouse, S, the office, T, and the caretaker's cottage, U. The warehouse was the real find of the fieldwork at Grovelands because for some reason it had not been opened for the sale of the products since 1927. The racks were full of the tiles, finials, ridges, ventilators and letter tiles which had been listed in the catalogues between the 1890s and the 1914–18 war. Plate 22, which shows ventilator ridge tiles, is typical of the storage racks in this warehouse. The various racks were photographed so that a complete record of the products was made whilst they still existed in a collection. The owners of the site sold off these tiles as 'antiques' before the warehouse was demolished! The office had been cleared of all its papers and these had been burnt with the exception of a few items—about 250kg (5 cwts.). The author went through these and rescued a lot of original design drawings for panels, for decorative work, for the letter tiles, and for the whole of Queen Victoria Street, Reading, which is a double-sided street built by Colliers entirely in terracotta and decorative moulded brickwork. These items were cleaned and sent to the drawings collection of the Royal Institute of British Architects. Other finds included the catalogues (and the drawings used to produce the catalogues). Some blocks from the catalogues were rescued as well as the 'Silchester Pottery' trade-mark stamp. This material is to be deposited in the local record office after its use in further research.

The records of the survey of Grovelands Brickworks have not been published and as yet remain in the author's possession. The main record of the survey is a large album of about 100 photographs put together from the 200 which were taken. Measurements of the kilns have been made and remain to be drawn up if publication at a later date warrants this. A register of known buildings using S. & E. Collier's products remains to be compiled but a start has been made on this. Documentary research in various record

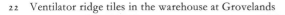

22 Ventilator ridge tiles in the warehouse at Grovelands

offices, architects' offices and builders' offices remains to be tackled if the fieldwork is to be amplified into a book about the brickworks. In terms of the fieldwork, nothing more could sensibly have been done without a large team of people measuring the buildings. However, the author maintains that in the case of a site such as this, the use of measured drawings would not greatly amplify the photographic record. All that now remains of the site is the war memorial at the gate which records on terracotta panels the names of the firm's dead in two world wars.

The survey of an area or unit in an emergency

The pressures on the use of land up and down the country at the present time are enormous. The result of these pressures is that industrial buildings and sites are frequently overwhelmed before they can be recorded in any way. This section is intended to give the fieldworker some guidance in how to set about recording a site in an emergency.

In the first instance, the industrial archaeologist, having learnt that the demolition of an industrial monument cannot be avoided, should evaluate the site. What are the uses of the site and the various buildings on it? Which buildings in the complex are crucial to the industry and which are ancillary —canteens, washrooms and the like? Whilst all the elements on the site are related to the industry, if the fieldworker's time is limited, he must concentrate on those which have most importance. Having determined the priorities for his examination and recording, the fieldworker should prepare a check-list for his work and should adhere to this list whilst at work.

Black and white photographs are the basic recording to be undertaken by the fieldworker when an emergency threatens an industrial site. Measured drawings, whilst desirable, are time consuming and so would have to be the last item tackled if there was time. Furthermore, as there will be no time for background research, the photographs must be as complete as possible. If parts of the buildings or plant are difficult to understand, then the photographs must be taken to explain the arrangement. When using the photographs after the recording has been completed, the fieldworker will have time to find out about the elements he did not previously understand.

To demonstrate the contents of an emergency survey the author is describing the work he did at Sonning Mill, Oxfordshire, and at the cooper's shop in Courage's brewery at Reading. The emergency in the case of Sonning Mill was caused by the opening of a large milling complex at Tilbury by the parent company. The company closed down their mills at Sonning and at Sharnbrook in Bedfordshire as soon as the port mill was underway. The company policy was to strip out the roller-milling equipment as soon as the mill closed down so that the mill could not exist in competition with their port mills. Knowing that the equipment was to be removed, the author was given permission to photograph this equipment during its last week of working. Only one day was available for this work. In the case of the cooperage at Courage's brewery, this was a closure of the cooper's shop because of the introduction of metal barrels. Here only one day was available for the work and, because this 'shop' was organized on a piece-work basis, only the morning was possible.

The author made arrangements to visit Sonning Mill and reported to the office on arrival. Whilst he had been given permission to do the recording, a further series of explanations were necessary. Owners—and employees—frequently cannot see the reasons for a fieldworker finding their buildings and plant interesting. Merely to describe one's intentions as 'industrial archaeology' does not always satisfy the questioners. It is useful to meet the person giving the permission, for then he can assess the dedication and concern of the fieldworker. After such a meeting the owner will usually want to take the industrial archaeologist round his factory or site to show him the various parts. The author, whilst welcoming this sort of assistance, goes round noting points made by the person conducting him but he does not do any of the recording work during such a tour. It is useful to explain to the owner at the outset that the fieldworker prefers to work on his own after being shown round, if this is the case. This enables a certain amount of analysis to be made without the interruptions, albeit well meant, of the owner. It also prevents working whilst being overlooked and one is not interrupted when concentrating on the various steps necessary to take a good photograph.

Sonning Mill is a large complex consisting of a late eighteenth-century weatherboarded mill of two storeys and an attic, to which was added the roller-mill plant and building of 1894, an extension of 1913 and the granary wing and silos of the 1920s. At the stage described, the author did not need to photograph the buildings as they were protected by the Planning Acts and were not threatened with destruction. The author concentrated on making a full record of the plant during which he examined and photographed every item of the '10 sack' roller plant. Unlike the conventional stone-grinding flour mill, the roller mill is in reality a complete machine with grain going in at one end and the sacks of flour and meal coming out at the other. The grain processes through the plant from one stage to the next without being bagged up or lifted about physically. After leaving one stage the meal is whisked to the next in a series of elevators. In photographing the plant, therefore, the author started at the input end and fol-

23   Heads of elevators in the attic storey, Sonning Mill

lowed the sequence through to the loading of sacks onto the company's lorry.

In some parts of Sonning Mill the machinery was very closely arranged and the fieldworker passing through those areas was reminded of Charles Chaplin passing through the machinery in his film *Modern Times*. Accordingly it was very difficult to take overall views of the machinery which could mean anything. Plate *23* shows this very clearly. In this plate the view was taken along the heads of some of the 32 elevators which passed from the

24　Elevators on grinding floor, Sonning Mill

attic down the various levels in the building. Plate 24 shows these elevators at the point at which they passed through the floor where the roller-grinding took place. The wheels on the left side of this picture are the control wheels of the roller-machines which lined this aisle. The glass panels enabled the operatives to see the way the elevators were running and to see if the correct weight of grain was being carried upwards. The author photographed the machinery in its individual items and also took a few photographs of the disposition of the machines when this was possible.

Plate 25 shows the roller-grinding machines on the roller-grinding floor (the second floor) at the upstream side of the area. The reader will see the several variations in the casings of these rolls, which related to the various jobs they were doing, and these were all photographed and recorded in relation to the work they were doing. Plate 26 is a photograph of an individual machine, in this case a purifier, on the third floor of the mill.

The number of photographs actually used as a record of the machinery amounted to 60. About 12 of these could be classed as overall views of the machinery spaces; the rest are of individual items. The Blackstone diesel engine and the two waterwheels were also recorded and photographs were taken of the machines in the repair bay, of the sack stencil and of the grain being delivered from a lorry to the silo. Since the machinery was removed from Sonning Mill, the architects for the developers of the site have prepared measured drawings of the mill and the whole of the complex.

The cooper's shop at Courage's brewery at Reading was a different proposition to record, for the problem was not one of the photography of machinery but of men, tools and methods used. The men had a row of work benches under the windows of a large steel-framed two-storey building. Each man had his own complete area of work bench and work space, which

25   Roller-grinding machines on grinding floor, Sonning Mill

26   Purifier on third floor, Sonning Mill

was jealously guarded. Apart from some powered machines provided by the brewery, all the tools were hand tools and were the property of the men themselves. These tools were largely obtained by the men during their apprenticeship, as the coopers had a strong guild arrangement which, although it is now numerically small, is still a controlling guild rather than a union. The author first of all photographed the men at work, as he could deal with the tools and the building after they had finished the day's stint. The men were photographed at each stage in the repair of the barrels and using each tool. Here the author made a bad mistake which is worth describing so that other fieldworkers are not similarly caught out. Plate 27 shows a copper at work cold-riveting an iron hoop on the bick iron. The author was using flash to arrest the movement of the man's hands but what he overlooked was the value of the natural light which was much stronger than the flash for that type of film and so the flight of the hand and hammer is blurred. The colour slides taken at the same time on very slow film have no movement.

    The record of men at work consists of 17 photographs. After these were

27   A cooper cold-riveting a hoop, Courage's Brewery, Reading

28   Bung-cutting machine in cooper's shop, Courage's Brewery, Reading

completed, the author photographed the work of those men who were not coopers on piece-work. The foreman was condemning barrels, marking up the defective staves and he also inserted the bungs into the repaired barrels. Another man was painting and branding the name of the brewery on the heads of the barrels. A third man was cutting up defective barrels which could not be re-used for beer for use as flower tubs. General views were then taken, including the machinery where possible. Plate *28* shows a view across the shop to the bung-cutting machine. The tools were photographed with a scale beside them and in pairs as far as possible so as to keep the various stages of the work together. Plate *29* shows the croze with the chiv to its right. The author was assisted by the men in every possible way, bearing in mind that they were on piece-work. At one point, without prompting, one of the men suddenly wove some of the traditional rush packing into a crown and was photographed wearing it—in spite of his embarrassment. This was a piece of the apprentice-to-master ceremony.

   The preceding two examples are typical of the problems with which the fieldworker may be called upon to deal at short notice. Quite clearly, other problems which may have to be faced make more or less the same demands. The fieldworker must analyse the needs of each site separately and work out each series of priorities, taking into account the importance of each item and the time and manpower available. Short cuts have to be taken or the industrial unit will not be adequately recorded. One short cut is that complex sites need not be measured. The large-scale Ordnance Survey maps at a scale of 1:1,250 or 1:2,500 can be used to produce large-scale plans of the monument. There are two methods of drawing these plans: one is to grid the large-scale map with a grid at, say, 10 metres square, and at the chosen scale of reproduction the 10 metres square grid is put on tracing paper. The various points are then plotted out on the plan, using the small squares on the map to transfer the information. Another way is to overlay the map of the site with a sheet of tracing paper, then place a pin in the approximate centre of the site. Then draw lines from the pin to salient features and extend them. Using a set of dividers 'walk' the distance from the pin to the feature by the number of steps equal to the ratio chosen— five steps to translate the 1:2,500 map to a 1:500 plan. Alternatively the feature can be fixed using measurements on a 1:2,500 and 1:500 scale. If this plan has been drawn for publication the fieldworker must remember that he has copyright obligations to the Ordnance Survey.

The distinction between the various forms of fieldwork study is obviously blurred. In spite of the depressing effect which some of these surveys must have on the fieldworker who has a concern for the past, they can be very rewarding and, if they proceed to completion and publication, the fieldworker will have the satisfaction of a job well done.

29   Croze and chiv at work bench in cooper's shop, Courage's Brewery, Reading

3. Reading the site or the monument

Many industrial archaeologists find the detective work necessary to read the remains on a site or of derelict industrial buildings very interesting. Whether one is faced with a 'lost' site or with buildings which have been partly demolished, there are many pointers which enable the fieldworker to understand the site properly. This chapter is designed to examine some of these pointers and to help with the extremely tricky subject of dating buildings.

The industrial archaeologist working on the subject of water power can have a fascinating time in those mining areas where water-powered haulage and pumping was used. In the Coniston Massif there are a great many leats serving the numerous waterwheel sites. For example, at Red Dell Beck the water was first led from a weir on the beck to serve a waterwheel at the ore-dressing works known as Red Dell works. This leat was about 450m (500 yards) long. At the works it was taken into a mill pond, which was built out on an embankment so that the waterwheel was overshot at the end of the embankment. Red Dell works was abandoned quite early in the nineteenth century in favour of the works at Paddy End on the Lever's Water Beck. However, its leat was extended to serve the larger waterwheel which worked the inclined plane up to the Bonser Level. The new wall of the leat, at the point at which it prevented the water from going into the Red Dell mill pond, is clearly visible. Thus one can see that the wheel for the Bonser Level was put in after the closure of the Red Dell works. The Bonser Level wheel was also served by water brought round Kennel Crag from the Lever's Water Beck and the two leats were joined in the mill pond built beside the incline. The sizes of the leats do not readily give the sizes of the wheels they drove. For example, without the auction documents it would not be possible to identify the sizes of the Red Dell waterwheel because there were no bearing points or pits for the wheel at this site. The Bonser Level wheel, however, is more easily read. Here the waterwheel was mounted in a wheel pit with the bearing plates at ground level. Providing the pit has not been distorted by earth movement, one can see the size of the wheel. Generally the width of the pit is 150mm (6 in.) larger than the waterwheel and the length is usually about 300mm (1 ft) greater than the diameter of the wheel at each end. On the opposite side of Red Dell Beck, and served with water taken out of Red Dell Beck below the Red Dell works, there was a 15·25m (50-ft) diameter wheel which provided the haulage in a shaft called Cobbler's Hole. Here there is a row of stone pillars which spans the space between a mill pond and the wheel pit. This row of pillars supported some sort of wooden launder. From the height of the pillars it is clear that the launder was taken to the top centre of the wheel but from the evidence on site there is no knowing whether the wheel was overshot or backshot. The row of bolts on the edge of the wheel pit shows that there was a timber sill along the whole length of the wheel and therefore, in addition to carrying the bearings, this sill must have supported a timber framework carrying the launder to the top centre of the wheel.

In agricultural areas streams frequently show evidence of watermill sites such as dams, wheel pits and the remains of buildings. Often these cannot be explained or confirmed by the evidence of adjacent settlements, and reference to the parish boundaries shown on the Ordnance Survey maps will show that a parish boundary has been 'stretched' to include a portion of the stream and the putative mill site. This was because each manor or parish had its own mill with the legal right to grind corn for that village only. For ease in control, therefore, the parish boundary was adjusted to include the mill. The layout of tracks, too, is indicative of a mill site. Footpaths would lead to the mill, or to a bridge which existed at the mill, so that the villagers could bring their corn to the mill or so that they could cross the water at that point.

The industrial archaeologist is familiar with the remains of railways which have recently been abandoned. The railbeds are often stony and therefore do not produce weeds and trees quickly. In the case of the long-abandoned railway the signs are harder to find. The narrow-gauge railway which ran around Buscot Park, for example, had only one earthwork—a shallow cutting about 200 yards long. Contemporary maps show the line quite clearly and one can then trace the line, as the gates which allowed the track to pass into each field can still be seen, as well as the pair of gates on opposite sides of the main road where there was a level crossing. Over the course of time the gates might have been replaced but they would not be moved to another site. The dairy at Buscot Park was served by the railway and its main floor stands above normal ground level so that the cans could be rolled straight into the trucks. The fact that a siding existed to the dairy can also be seen by the way the road to the dairy comes off the road which was built beside the main length of the railway.

In some areas the presence of plateways is well known and here the precise route can often be followed for miles, although in places there are now no visible remains. From Hereford a plateway runs more or less south to serve other plateways in Monmouthshire. The route is marked by embankments and cuttings, with the obvious sites of some bridges marked by gaps in the embankments. Searching can bring to light some of the sleeper blocks now used as paving for gate openings and the like. In Northumberland there are many railway or plateway tracks which were shown on the early maps—such as Greenwood's of 1829—which are still in use as cart tracks or footpaths. In some instances the very straight alignments show there to have been inclines worked with cable haulage and often the foundations of engine house can be seen at the ends of the runs. At Seaton Sluice and Hartley there was a series of plateways or early railways which ran down to the harbour from neighbouring coal mines. One embankment crosses the park of Seaton Delaval Hall to the edge of a cliff above the Seaton Burn. It is known to have crossed to the other side of the valley to pass down to the harbour. Here, on the banks, can be seen stone blocks with deep 200mm × 200mm (9 in. × 9 in.) sinkings in them. These were the padstones on which a wooden viaduct had been built.

Long-lost canals can be traced from their remains. Parallel with the railway between Taunton and Tiverton Junction there are lengths of bank which gradually diminish only to start again with a step of about 8 or 10 ft. These are lengths of canal and the step marks the site of locks on the Grand Western Canal. The Wilts and Berks Canal, which was abandoned at the end of the last century, can be traced in several places where it runs parallel to the railway between Wooton Basset and Chippenham in Wiltshire. The more obvious stretches still consist of two lines of mature trees with a dense infill of bushes and reeds between them. In one stretch, until quite recently, one could see where the canal had been 'bulldozed' out so that the fields had taken the land back again but the brick accommodation bridges remained. Also on the line of the Wilts and Berks Canal there are groups of cottages which stand parallel to the canal line and out of place in respect of the adjacent roads and which can only be explained in the context of the canal they served.

The remains of windmills can often be seen on the ground. It is always particularly important to look for them if one is looking at aerial photographs. At Stanbridge in Bedfordshire there is a brick tower mill which is now a house but 200 yards to the east there is a low mound in a field which appears to overlie the ridge-and-furrow field system. An aerial photograph, taken with evening light to cast long shadows, shows very clearly how the mound, and the trench which was used to provide the material to raise the mound, were cut out of the corner of the communal field. This must, therefore, have been the mound on which a post mill was built and the diameter is large enough to have carried the mill and the path of the tip of the tail pole. If the mound had been a burial barrow the ridge and furrow would have been cut over the top of it. In a housing estate in Hartley in Northumberland there is a street called Mill Way. The precise site of the windmill is identified by a 750mm (2 ft 6 in.) high stone wall built in a circle 6m (20 ft) in diameter. The name and the wall enable one to identify the site and illustrations in the local record office give details of type and size. Another clue in connection with towers thought to be windmills is the presence of doors at exactly opposite points in the walls. This is particularly the case with the short towers of a more primitive type where the sails came close to the ground. The reason is easy to see, as if there was only one door and the wind was in that direction, then the sails would pass in front of the door and prevent the miller from getting in or out of the mill.

In the north, horse wheel sites are marked by the presence of a shaped addition to the barns. Even though the machinery in the horse wheel house has gone, one can tell whether it was an engine with an overhead gear or had a gear at low level. The former would show the fixing points for a top bearing on the roof truss and the latter would show only as a blocked opening at low level in the barn wall. However, other sites, particularly of winding engines driven by horses, can be found in mining areas or outside the vent shafts of railway tunnels. There is a very clear site beside an existing copper-mine shaft in the Tilberthwaite basin below Wetherlam in the Coniston Fells. Dr Michael Lewis records a similar situation by a tunnel vent on the Festiniog railway. Subsequent excavation on the site showed the base of the three stone pillars supporting the frame on which the winding drum and horse arm were pivoted.

The industrial archaeologist will need to build up a personal knowledge, which can only come from experience, of the way in which the evidence of a building's changes can be seen. Frequently mills, or other industrial buildings, are altered and the industrial archaeologist will want to determine the extent of these alterations. For example, the corn mill, Upper Mill at Longparish in Hampshire, which dates from the early nineteenth century, has evidence of two major structural changes. The brickwork up to the head of the first-floor windows is a dark-blue brick and the next storey of brickwork is in a pale-red brick. The division between the bricks is so clear cut, with no running in of one brick into another at courses, that the addition must be a distinct process of building. At the south end of the mill, on the opposite side of the waterwheel away from the gear space, an extension has been added in weatherboard on timber framing. This is shown to be a later addition as the wall which separates the mill space from this is as thick as the north wall of the mill, whereas if it was no more than an internal wall it would have been only 9 in. thick and not the present 18 in. thick. Changes in the brick, or in the way the stone has been dressed, are a good indication of additions. Windows are not necessarily changed when used in new additions. If the originals were made of wood these could have been copied and if they were cast iron the patterns would have existed in local foundries for a long time and could easily have been repeated.

Evidence of changes in machinery will be visible to the experienced industrial archaeologist. For example, the corn mill, Heron Mill at Beetham in Cumbria, has clearly had its earlier waterwheel changed for a larger one which still exists. This is shown by the fact that the bearing of the present wheel is at a higher level than that of its predecessor which stood on a shelf below the present sill carrying the existing bearing. The present wooden launder stands on the top of a stone wall and goes into the mill to drive the wheel pitchback. The supporting wall has a line showing an addition about 1·25 m (4 ft) below the top and this is marked by an opening into the building at this level. The previous waterwheel, therefore, was smaller because the tail race discharges directly into the river and so could not have been altered and with a lower bearing the radius was therefore shorter—but the width of the wheel remained the same.

In a similar way, with experience, the industrial archaeologist working in a mill will readily spot the changes in the millwork. Iron shafts which replaced earlier wooden shafts can be seen because the hub has to have a supplementary cast-iron hub box made to make up the difference between the narrow iron shaft and the larger wooden shaft. Mill owners were naturally conservative and only replaced the minimum when things broke down and it is for this reason that so many mills contain millwork with both wood and iron gearing arrangements. Water-driven corn mills present these changes rather obviously but other industries have similar facets. The mill at Rode (Plate 6) has changed from a blanket mill to a corn mill and back to a blanket mill. The turbine for the later driving of the blanket mill stands in a waterway beside the waterwheel. The waterwheel still has a complete hurst frame beside it but has no machinery above the basement level containing the hurst frame. The siting of the machines must have changed because the pattern of blocked and unblocked windows has clearly been changed.

Dating industrial buildings without actual date plates is not easy. There are no sure pointers which can be used to an accuracy of less than 50 years. The obvious architectural styles do have their parallels in the industrial buildings. Mill owners, who were the *nouveau riche* of the eighteenth century, embellished their factories in the classical style of the period. Copy books existed for the joinery and the general details and these were used in the design of the factories as well as for the houses. Arkwright's Cressbrook Mill shows this: the pediment, cupola and quoins are as obviously correctly used here as they would be on the large house in the park such as nearby Chatsworth. Good architectural textbooks will enable the fieldworker to put general dates on buildings from these stylistic features. The Lancashire cotton boom of the early twentieth century, for instance, produced very distinctive buildings in hard red brick with Edwardian classical details, usually embellishing only the windows or towers.

There are details which can give only a clue to the earliest date at which the building could have been carried out. Patent fireproof constructions of cast-iron columns and beams supporting brick-arch floors cannot have been built before the 1790s. However, cast-iron columns remained in use until the end of the nineteenth century. Cast-iron windows were not used much before 1800 and remained in use until the introduction of the galvanized mild-steel window in this century. In industrial buildings the actual style of the cast-iron window remained extremely constant with the low arched head and the centre four panes which opened.

In mills with simple structures there are other signs of date. Cast-iron rainwater goods did not replace lead much before 1800, so lead down pipes and heads would indicate a general eighteenth century date. Often one finds lead rainwater heads in place, although the down pipe has been replaced in cast iron. The classical window frame with 12 panes of glass can give some indication of date. When the window bars and meeting rail are thin with fine mouldings, the window is likely to be pre-1830, whereas the heavier mouldings on wider window bars are later than that. Similarly the window with only four panes, two in the upper sash and two in the lower sash, is indicative of the change from window glass which was blown to the glass which could be made in large sheets. This was also after the 1830s or 1840s. If the structural timbers have been sawn and not adzed to shape, this indicates that they were eighteenth century rather than earlier. If the timbers show the circular marks—evidence that a circular saw was used—this would suggest a date later than 1830. One cannot make hard and fast rules about any of this dating. Reciprocating saws are still used in some yards and these would give parallel marks across the timber but the same marks could equally have been left by hand sawyers using a saw pit. Brick sizes cannot be taken as a firm indication of date as bricks vary in size in different parts of Britain. The northern type of brick gave 4 courses to 330 mm (13 in.) and the southern type gave 4 courses to 300 mm (12 in.). Now new brick sizes have been made universal by metrication. The old 'Tudor' two-in. brick was still being made in Reading in the twentieth century!

Only experience will enable the fieldworker to apply any rules to the reading of sites and buildings with certainty. In his early visits to sites he will have to discuss his findings with others to enable him to have any sure knowledge of what has happened to a site. Lack of knowledge must not deter the fieldworker from undertaking the work, for only by going out into the field will he be able to build up any experience of his subject.

4. Background research as an aid to the fieldworker

The industrial archaeologist will need to use background research in connection with his fieldwork. He will use some research as an aid to finding sites; some at an intermediate stage during the fieldwork; and some after the fieldwork has been completed—to aid his understanding of the results. The purpose of this chapter is to analyse the background material available and to help the industrial archaeologist to choose the right material for his particular project.

There are many institutions which the industrial archaeologist can use for his research and to gain information about the particular problem on which he is working. The first place to look for material would be the local record office or reference library. These usually have very good coverage of their local area but not necessarily of the fieldworker's particular study. The staff usually have knowledge of other sources which will help the worker if their own shelves fail to carry the right documents. The industrial archaeologist should remember to deposit in the local record office any material which he has rescued. If there is a local museum its staff may be able to help but some local museums may have a bias away from industrial archaeology. The opening hours of museums are published in *Museums and Galleries in Great Britain and Northern Ireland* which is issued every year and this also gives the range of the collections.

For the industrial archaeologist able to get to London the opportunities are excellent. The British Museum Reading Room and Map Room are ideal places in which to do much private research. The Reading Room can only be used on production of a reader's card but the facilities of the Map Room are available on application at its counter. However, if one wishes to consult maps of a larger scale than 1:10 560 (6 in. to a mile) they should be ordered at least 24 hours in advance and precise details of the requirements given. The library of the Science Museum in South Kensington is excellent for the industrial archaeologist but as it is not a copyright library not every book required is in stock there. When using libraries, map rooms or museum facilities it is a great help to know exactly what one wants.

Maps

The most important documents for an industrial archaeologist, when he is working on an area survey or on an overall survey of an industry, are the maps of the area in question. The fieldworker should own and use the 1-in. Ordnance Survey map, or if his area is not too large, the 1:25 000 (2½-in.) Ordnance Survey map. This will enable him to get about in his search for industrial monuments and will give him the National Grid references to record the objects he has found. In his preliminary search into the distribution and siting of the monuments on which he is working the fieldworker should use the earlier editions of the 1:10 560 (6-in.) or 1:2500 (25-in.) maps. He will probably not be able to afford to buy them and should consult them in the local library or museum. The early maps do not contain National Grid references, so if one wishes to note the site of an object one has to refer to it as 'so many yards distant from the parish church in a north-westerly direction'. A 150mm (6-in.) ruler will do the scaling off and the compass direction can be done by eye. In dealing with the maps of a whole county it is essential to start in one corner (north-west) and to work through to the opposite corner in a systematic fashion. Keep strictly to the contents of the parishes; for preservation reasons it is important to know the parish or township in which a monument stands.

In the nineteenth century the Ordnance Survey published some town plans at a scale of 1:500. These plans are extremely useful, for not only do they detail the uses to which complete units are put but they also label individual items of equipment which appear in the plan. The present-day equivalent of this scale is 1:1250 and these plans exist for several large towns. The industrial archaeologist will need to see what is available in his local record office. A valuable source of information which can be seen at the office of the Ordnance Survey in Southampton is the collection of surveyors' notebooks for the Ordnance Survey which go back to the first surveys in the early part of the nineteenth century.

The industrial archaeologist has many other maps to which he can refer and which may be of use to him in addition to the Ordnance Survey maps. Map-making, based on valid surveys, dates back a long way but the first maps which can be of any real use to the fieldworker are the county surveys produced in the eighteenth century. Maps such as Chapman and Andre's *Map of Essex* of 1774, Andrews' and Drury's *Map of Wiltshire* of 1773, and Benjamin Donn's *Map of Devon* of 1765 are typical of these. Here the principal towns are all shown with some accuracy in their layout, prominent features such as windmills, gibbets and the like are depicted and interesting objects such as brick kilns and the different types of watermills are also shown. Road maps such as Ogilby's *Britannia* of 1675 and Bowen's *Britannia Depicta* of 1720 give a great deal of information about the buildings and activities adjacent to the roads. Using *Britannia Depicta* as a cross-check on some mill sites in north Oxfordshire, the author was able to confirm the presence of windmills which were only 'hearsay' sites. The accuracy of the dimensioning on these maps is sometimes suspect as it relied on the 'way-wiser' to obtain the distances. A waywiser is a measuring machine which counts the revolutions of a large wheel of known circumference which the surveyor pushes in front as he goes along the road and they are still used in a modern form. Later surveys of counties, such as those of Greenwood at $1:126\,720$ ($\frac{1}{2}$ in.) or $1:63\,360$ (1 in. to the mile), are even more useful, for although they were printed at the time of the first Ordnance Surveys, they often contained items which the Ordnance Survey maps neglected.

There are also other maps which are particularly useful to the industrial archaeologist. Estate maps are often to be found in the archive offices of local authorities, where they have been placed on the closure of a particular estate or solicitor's office, or in the estate records. The author was greatly helped in his production of the book, *The Mills of the Isle of Wight*, by being able to use the maps in the muniment room of Winchester College. Here, each mill owned by the college had been surveyed by professional land surveyors and beautiful maps had been drawn in black ink on white paper and bound up into volumes. The changes in the shape of the mills were easily read from these surveys because they had been drawn prior to the change in milling patterns which occurred on the island about 1793. Tithe maps for the parishes are particularly useful as they describe and identify the various types of building, owner and land holding in each area. In some towns the maps produced by the insurance companies are useful. The maps in the record office at Reading show everything in considerable detail. The actual layout of equipment in the breweries is readily discernible and the numbers of horse wheels in each of the smaller sites is noted and their size written on the plans.

In the case of undertakings such as the railways or the canals, the British Transport Historical Records Office at 66 Porchester Road, Paddington, contains the maps and plans of the railways and canals and their buildings. Local authority town planning and building inspectors' offices may contain maps and plans of buildings erected since the inception of the Public Health Acts but a lot of this material has been destroyed because of the space it took up or because of the salvage drive during the 1939–45 war.

Guide books

The industrial archaeologist may enjoy his research into his chosen subject more when he begins to look at nineteenth-century guide books. These are full of interest, much of it irrelevant, some useful and some frankly humorous. The road books could be described as the first true guide books. In these, their authors described the features to be seen on either side of the principal roads as one drove along. Many of the items listed were included in the hope that the owners would buy copies of the books. These road books are typified by *Paterson's Roads* or Cary's *Great Roads*. Similar volumes were produced in the early days of the railway and Coghlan's *The Iron Road Book* of 1838 is a good example. The information contained in these volumes was often scrappy but with diligent reading it can be useful to the industrial archaeologist. For example, in column 274 of Cary's *Great Roads*, the reference to Paddington is useful to those doing work on the Grand Junction Canal: 'Paddington, at, a Branch of the Grand Junction Canal, on which are established Passage Boats during the summer season to Greenford Green, near Harrow'. This note was published in 1821. *Paterson's Roads* is even more explicit and this paragraph from the description of Reading is useful in its picture of the trading position of the town: 'The town is divided into 2 parts by the river Kennet, which forms several excellent wharves in its passage, and is navigable westward to Newbury, Froxfield etc; the Kennet and Avon Canal is also of considerable advantage to the town, as it opens a communication between the Thames and the Severn.' The same volume also has a concern for pollution which, written 150 years ago, seems remarkably contemporary. On page 275 in the section taking the reader through Weardale one reads: 'In proceeding from Wolsington to Stanhope, large parcels of lead are seen lying by the sides of the road, which intimate the commencement of the lead district, as do also the blue unwholesome vapours that arise from the smelting-mills at Bollihope, on the common'. Modern guide books such as A. Wainwright's seven volumes *A Pictorial Guide to the Lakeland Fells* make enjoyable reading and, whilst not deliberately singling out industrial sites for attention, do deal with them. *Book Four: The Southern Fells* deals at some length with the visible remains of the copper industry and slate quarrying of the Coniston Fells. The inclusion does not mean that Wainwright has studied these remains but he has put them on the map so that visitors can avoid them or look for them as they wish.

Directories

Directories of various places have been in existence for about 200 years and form a source of information on trades and tradesmen for the industrial archaeologist. Whilst the directories are excellent, they must be treated with caution. Although many directories list everybody and all the trades practising in an area, others only included people on the payment of a fee. Again, for some reason or another, tradespeople did not get entries in every edition. In the case of watermills, for example, the mill might be in the process of being re-built and not at work. In another situation the owner might be ill and so the information form was not returned. If a mill was not trading but only working privately for an estate or a farmer, then there was no entry.

Taking the above cautionary note into account, how does one go about consulting directories? The most important point at which to start is by consulting Jane E. Norton's *Guide to the National and Provincial Directories* or *The London Directories 1677–1855* by C. W. F. Goss. These list all the known directories and so one can find out which ones exist for a particular area. Some directories such as Kelly's list the tradespeople in the entry for each town or in a large block of trades at the end of the volume. The contemporary equivalent is the telephone directory with its 'yellow pages' of tradespeople and services at the back. With the exception of unlisted numbers, the telephone directory is much the most accurate of all directories. Like guide books, directories can make interesting reading. For instance, the notes on South Shields in White's *Directory and Gazetteer of Durham and Northumberland* published in 1828 contain the following entry for the author's great-great-grandfather: 'Major Francis, mariner, Pleasant Place'. Entries like this can be assembled for all the mariners in South Shields, in County Durham or on the Tyne. Similar entries exist for the millwrights, millers, etc. If one is doing a survey of the whole of an industry in a particular area, the directory is probably the first source document which should be consulted.

'Victoria History of the Counties of England'

At an early stage in his research the industrial archaeologist will discover the *Victoria History of the Counties of England*, initiated, as the name suggests, at the end of the nineteenth century. Not all the counties have been covered and as the volumes are still being produced, obviously the coverage is variable. Only the most recent volumes pay reasonable attention to industrial history. Those volumes which deal with areas such as Birmingham give industrial history because it is so intimately bound up with the area.

The histories are not always easy to use, as the breakdown into hundreds —a medieval political boundary—is not readily understood nowadays as the hundred names and boundaries are not normally known. There is also a great deal of medieval material in the books drawn from the cartuleries, court deeds and charters. In many instances this has been printed in preference to social or economic history. In the summary volumes the industrial archaeologist may find chapters on social or industrial history but they form no more than the briefest of guides.

A similar series of volumes, working to a different specification, are those of the *Royal Commission on Historical Monuments*. When first published they were limited to buildings dating from before 1714 but now include certain buildings of more recent date. In the volumes produced since the war of 1939–45 there has been an increasing tendency to deal with industrial monuments. For example, Telford's Conway suspension bridge of 1826 and Robert Stephenson's tubular bridge of 1848 are described in *Caernarvonshire Vol. 1 East* published by the Royal Commission in 1956. Perhaps more surprising are the references to minor industrial monuments such as that for Gwenddar Mill in Llangelynin. The references to mills in the Anglesey volume and in the Cambridge volume were prepared by Rex Wailes who was industrial monuments consultant to the then Ministry of Works.

Local histories

Local histories should be used cautiously by the industrial archaeologist for they are often seriously inaccurate. Many people who write as local historians are excellent workers who can combine an accurate use of research material with a good understanding of the objects which they have seen in the field. A larger class, particularly in the period before the 1939–45 war, were apt to use their research as their only source of information and were not prepared to get their boots muddy in carrying out field studies. The industrial archaeologist must, therefore, proceed with caution. The author found a slim pamphlet dealing with a foundry which he knew, where a waterwheel was built in 1874 to drive the cupola furnace fans. This pamphlet was about the use of the site as a smithy during the 1730s and it was stated that the waterwheel was installed to operate a tilt hammer. The day books of this smithy in that period show that the smithy would have needed no power other than that of the smith's arm. The range of work was too small and the financial return was too insignificant to warrant a water-driven hammer.

Many volumes are excellent. Aiken's *Description of the Country 30 to 40 miles round Manchester*, published in 1795, and Bulmer's *History, Topography and Directory of Furness and Cartmel*, are good examples of the larger studies. Almost any page in Aiken's *Description* will give material of use to the industrial archaeologist. For example these two sentences from the page on Leigh: 'Lime is got at Bedford near Leigh, of a kind like that of Sutton, hardening speedily under water, and therefore fit for lining reservoirs, and the like purposes. It is much used on the Duke of Bridgewater's canal.' During the nineteenth century many local antiquarian and archaeological societies were formed. These often have very useful material in their transactions or journals. Whilst these do not seem to be an obvious source of information, their usefulness should not be overlooked. While the author was tracing the watermills on the river Cherwell in mid-Oxfordshire, he was certain that he had found a building which had been a mill, although to all intents and purposes it was now a range of cottages. Reference to the Oxford Historical Society's 1893 volume, *Three Oxfordshire Parishes— Kidlington, Yarnton, Begbroke*, indentified the building as Thrup Mill. It had been converted from its milling use in 1790, when the Oxford and Birmingham Canal purchased the mill and its mill pond from the parish and used the water to supply the canal.

Deposited plans

Deposited plans form a valuable source of information in relation to works requiring an Act of Parliament. They can be found for all road works, railway or canal construction or the provision of pipelines and reservoirs for water supplies. In their basic forms, deposited plans are statements of the land ownership over which the proposed services were to be run. If the plans are properly documented, they can also form a good record of the lie of the land and of the relationship with other industrial users. When the author first discovered, for himself, the lost but exciting North Walsham and Dilham Canal, which runs from the river Ant at Dilham in Norfolk through North Walsham to a terminal at Antingham some eight miles from the start, he was conscious of the peculiar relationship between the water-mills on the canal and the locks. He first of all recorded all the important items on the canal—the locks, bridges, wharves and the toll cottage—and walked as much of the canal as the absence of a towing path of any sort would permit. This survey left the question of the mills and their relationship with the canal locks unresolved and so he sought the deposited plans in the County Record Office in Norwich. The deposited plans had been prepared twice: first in 1811 and again in 1812. Why they had to be re-submitted is not known but it is likely that the mill owners objected to the first set of plans. The engineer who signed the plans was J. Millington of

Hammersmith. The first scheme proposed a canal with equal rises at each of the locks and with the locks bearing little relationship to the mill ponds. The second scheme (which was built) put locks in a correct relationship to the mill dams. Although the river Ant still runs down the valley, the canal is a true canal and not a navigation because the river channel was too tortuous and there was too little water in it.

The first mill, Dilham Mill, has a long mill pond. The canal runs parallel to it and the lock occurs at the point at which the canal joins the river where it opens out into the mill pond. The other mills are served in the usual way with the lock rising at the mill dam adjacent to the mill. The canal has taken over from the river completely and the deposited plans show how the original canal line varied from the river line as in many places the river bed has disappeared. The deposited plans show the names of land owners and on this set one finds the family name of Cubitt associated with Dilham Mill and with several of the fields around the canal. This is, of course, the family home of Sir William Cubitt. Obviously deposited plans will give the industrial archaeologist insight into the arrangements which created the particular monument in which he is interested. They can also give a great deal of information about the area surrounding the monument.

Catalogues

The industrial archaeologist may find the catalogues which are available in the local record office or reference library a valuable source of information. If the catalogues are those issued by the industry on which he is working, he can see how the various parts of the factory were related to the finished product. If, on the other hand, they are machinery suppliers' catalogues, then these will enable the industrial archaeologist to understand the layout of the industrial unit and to identify the machinery used.

These are the more obvious ways in which to make use of catalogues but nineteenth-century catalogues are often full of other information. The firm may have used an engraving of the works in the front of the catalogue in order to show its size. Associated companies may also be listed and so the fieldworker can find further examples of the same trade or related trades. Often, too, the writer of the catalogue included copies of letters praising the work of the firm for which it was produced. An example of this is the catalogue of John Wallis Titt of Warminster issued in 1911. The letters of reference for the wind engine at Crux Easton (Plate 4) read as follows:

April 7th 1892
Estate Office, Highclere Park, Newbury.

Dear Sir,

The Wind Engine and Pumps you erected at Crux Easton have worked steadily and well since completion, and are, I think, in every way a sound job.

Yours truly J. A. Rutherford
Agent to the Earl of Caernarvon.

P.S. The above well in this case is 410 feet [124m] deep.

Crux Easton, Whitchurch, Hants.
August 13th 1894.

Dear Sir,

Your Wind Engine for Pumping and Grinding Corn on this Farm, has done good service. Besides Pumping Water it grinds frequently eight to ten sacks of Corn per day. It is a cheap and most valuable improvement to this place.

Mr. J. W. Titt   Yours truly S. G. Wake.

Although these appear to be solicited references, they are still full of useful information. In the case of the Crux Easton wind engine, the author saw the reference in the Museum of English Rural Life in Reading one morning and found the remains the same afternoon!

In the case of Collier's brickworks described in Chapter 2 the author found the tile catalogue in a rubbish heap. This has enabled him to go round and find the distribution of Collier's products. It is also the catalogue which was used by the office to fix the piece-work rate for the production of the tile, finial or decorative piece in relation to the selling price of the item. This is in code, using letters instead of figures. Clearly the management did not expect the workers to be able to crack the code and see the end profit.

In addition to catalogues produced for sales' purposes many firms have produced their own histories. These have usually been written for some sort of anniversary and usually detail the various stages which the firm has gone through up to that point. These volumes often have illustrations showing the various stages in the development of the factory and frequently have photographs of a range of products and state where they were used.

The industrial archaeologist may not wish to look at catalogues or the histories of firms before he begins his fieldwork. It is probably better if he consults these when he has reached some point of interpretation which creates a problem in reading the site. If a particular catalogue is not readily available the fieldworker should not delve too deeply to find it.

Auction documents and deeds

One very rewarding area of research for the industrial archaeologist during the course of his fieldwork is auction documents and deeds which relate to the site with which he is concerned. These can exist in the local record office, the land agent's office or in solicitors' offices. If an industrial site changed hands just prior to its demolition, then it should be possible to obtain copies of the auction and sale documents from the agents who handled the sale. When the author was working on Collier's brickworks and the Tilehurst Potteries in Reading, he obtained a copy of the auction document from the agent. In the case of the Tilehurst Potteries, each building is identified in the sale and its size is noted, together with its use. When the sites were photographed by the author, the works had been closed for at least a year and so the loose equipment had gone and it was difficult to establish the use of a particular area.

The sale documents of the Coniston and Tilberthwaite Mines for the auction sale held on 3 August 1875 still exist and are extremely helpful to the fieldworker examining the area. The description of the machinery and plant at the Coniston Mines shows how valuable such a document can be:

> One water wheel 21 feet [6·40m] diameter attached to the crushing mill and screens
>
> Crushing mill with two pairs of rollers
>
> Hoppers, screens, and elevators
>
> Two water wheels one 12 ft [3·65m] and one 13 ft [3·96m] diameter attached to the jigging machines
>
> Sixteen jigging machines, with line shafting, sieves, and troughs complete
>
> One water wheel 17 feet [5·18m] diameter
>
> Three platforms and hoists for unloading waggons
>
> Tramway 270 yards [247m] long laid from the crushing mill to the lower floors to take ore to the stamps with permanent rails
>
> 2 iron waggons ditto
>
> Horse level 1880 yards [1700m] long, laid with rails permanently from upper floors to the deep mine
>
> 10 iron waggons used on ditto
>
> 1 new water wheel, 32 feet [9·75m] diameter, attached to a saw bench in shop, with tables and 3 circular saws
>
> Shafting pullies and driving belts.

Of course this was being sold as a going concern and so there had to be a full description of the works to enable the purchasers to know what their capital equipment was going to be and how much new capital would be required. In fact there was not a great deal added to the mines after this time.

The industrial archaeologist may find himself spending several fruitless hours looking through deeds if he is seeking a guide to the history of an industrial monument. He will need to know something of the people and dates with which he is concerned in order to get the right information and not to miss the basic facts. The deeds of an industrial property are much more important to the social historian and economist. In the Cumberland County Record Office in Carlisle there are the deeds of the Low Mill at Alston in Cumberland (High Mill, not Low Mill, was the one designed by John Smeaton in his capacity as Consultant to the Greenwich Hospital). The deeds date from 1761 to 1903 and there are 32 individual documents in this group. There are only four or five which detail the sale or transfer of the mill from one owner to another; the rest deal either with the mortgaging of the mill or the taking of partners or joint owners. For the economic historian the interest lies in the value of the mill, the rental of the tenancies and the mortgage rates. The other deeds give details of how, in 1903, the sale of the mill could not be concluded—the new owner paid a small proportion on account and had eight months in which to pay the rest or pay interest at 4 per cent thereafter. For the industrial archaeologist the deeds demonstrate how the water was protected and secured, how the land was bought in to provide housing for workers and how partnerships were organized. The most important fact was that the first recorded purchase of the land on which the corn mill was then built was dated 1621. The stage at which deeds would be used by the industrial archaeologist is clearly when he is assembling material prior to publication. The labour of using these documents would not be justified in an early stage prior to fieldwork. The fieldworker, too, must not be drawn into interesting but fruitless and irrelevant research into deeds.

Postcards, photographs and engravings

Postcards, photographs and engravings are still quite cheap, so the industrial archaeologist will possibly wish to own those related to his own interests or to the monument on which he is working. However, it is not possible for him to collect everything, so he should make use of local collections when they exist. As with some of the other forms of documentation, these give a great deal of information which helps with the interpretation of finds on site.

Photographs can be found which date from the 1840s or 1850s and postcards which date from the 1890s. These, and stereographic photo pairs, are often very sharp and detailed and the information they carry is useful for the industrial archaeologist. Frequently photographs were taken for the content of the view and not as artistic studies and often the photographer regarded himself as a recorder and not as an artist. The collections of the work of Henry Taunt, who worked in Oxford between 1860 and 1920, which exist at the central libraries in Reading and Oxford, or those of Francis Frith, covering the latter half of the nineteenth century, show how useful the photograph can be. In the Taunt collection there is a photograph of about 1880 which shows the brickfield at Culham beside the Thames. All that remains now is the cliff formed by digging the clay and a single 'Newcastle' kiln. The photograph shows that the bricks were air dried in the open without any form of hack shed. At that time there was a single updraught kiln and a wharf on the river for the unloading of coal and the loading of bricks. This is a considerable help in reading the remains on site. There are lots of places of which photographs can still be found and it is worth using these when possible.

The use of aerial photography as a tool in archaeology was first put to a practical test in the years following the 1914–18 war. In the war primitive interpretative photography from the air enabled opposing sides to see what was going on at the front line and in the rear fortifications. Since that time a series of large aerial photographic collections has been built up. The professional firm of Aerofilms maintains a library in Albemarle St in London that can be consulted by members of the public. There is also a collection of aerial surveys at Cambridge University. Both these collections are large but books of their photographs are published from time to time. Aerial photographs can be used to advantage when studying the remains of obsolete industries: for instance when looking for the remains of bell pits dug by medieval iron miners, colliers or quarrymen. Aerial photographs would be particularly useful in examining water power sites in an area like the Coniston Fells.

Engravings, whilst extremely useful, have to be consulted with care. Sometimes they were mirror images of the real thing. For example, Birkett Foster's engraving of Holy Street Mill, Chagford, is accurate but it happens to be back to front. Wolvey, in Warwickshire, (Plate *30*) did have windmills, according to the first edition of the Ordnance Survey, but this is a well-executed engraving of it showing four windmills and the village street, which is, in fact, an engraving of Montmartre. Comparison with a

WOLVEY, WARWICKSHIRE.

30   Engraving entitled 'Wolvey Warwickshire'. This is, in fact, an engraving of the mills of Montmartre

photograph of Montmartre taken in 1842 shows that the engraving and the photograph were taken from the same viewpoint. Readers of Francis Klingender's *Art and the Industrial Revolution* will realize immediately the difference between those engravings which are pure reportage in the style set by *The Illustrated London News* and those which are meant to be artistic and which therefore use artist's licence in putting the scene on paper. Finden's *Ports and Harbours of Great Britain* is a volume of engravings in which the artistic licence adds dramatically to many of the scenes but others are fairly straightforward. Whilst they can be used to demonstrate the content of a view, engravings cannot be used with any accuracy to describe in detail any particular object.

The preceding pages have shown some of the material available for the fieldworker in his research. With experience he will find other sources which can help him. However exciting some of this background material may be, the fieldworker must not allow this material to become more important than the search for evidence and remains on site. The archives must only be a tool in the process of discovery and must not become an over-riding interest for the industrial archaeologist.

5. Measured drawings of industrial buildings

A measured drawing of a building is a drawing made to scale in plan section and elevation, or to another form of projection, from measurements taken on site. In many situations a measured drawing is the most valuable record which can be made. Such a drawing enables a building to be studied in depth and can be used as a research tool if the changes in the use of a building and the various alterations in its fabric have been recorded. This is, of course, particularly important if a building is to be demolished after measured drawings have been made. In some instances good measured drawings can be used to form part of the construction set of drawings if a building is to be restored or repaired.

The question of scale is a very difficult one for the industrial archaeologist. Britain is a country which had an imperial (feet and inches) system of measurement until the early 1970s and which has now gone over to the metric system. There are therefore two types of measurement open to the fieldworker. The official method is to measure everything in metric dimensions in which the unit of measurement is the millimetre, and the fieldworker then draws out his buildings in scales of 1:100, 1:50 or 1:20. The alternative method is to measure in feet and inches and to draw to scales of 1:100, 1:50 or 1:20. To do this the fieldworker should use a boxwood or ivorine scale, called an RIBA Scale B, which can be obtained quite cheaply from drawing office shops. The RIBA Scale B has feet and inches scales engraved on it to the metric ratios 1:100, 1:50, 1:20 etc. Drawings should then carry scales in both metres and feet which will make them universally readable. Metric has disadvantages in the measurement of existing buildings because the units cannot be rounded off. A simple 4 in. × 3 in. cross section on a piece of timber becomes 101mm × 76mm in metric. Measurements of an existing building should be taken to the nearest centimetre, but to ensure greater accuracy gearing etc. should be measured in millimetres. The industrial archaeologist's experience will dictate which system he uses. What is important is that industrial buildings should be measured.

The author has illustrated this chapter with his own work where he has measured his examples in the imperial system. The same methods of measurement apply to the use of the metric system. The points he makes are the same whichever system of measurement is used.

The ideal number of persons on a team preparing measurements is three, but that must not deter the individual who is faced with the need to prepare measurements for a small unit. The measurement of a workman's cottage is quite within the ability of a single person, and it is relatively easy for him to produce an accurate series of drawings. The quality of the measured drawings which result from the survey of an industrial building will depend on the experience and skills of the team involved.

The decision to prepare measured drawings will depend on several factors. The first is the importance of the industrial unit in its own industry or area. The second is the building and its value in terms of the industrial tradition in the field of building. (A unique structure would certainly merit the preparation of measured drawings and any remaining machinery should also be included showing its precise position.) The third is the lack of documentary evidence of the industry concerned. This applies mainly to nineteenth-century structures. No one would need to prepare measured drawings of huge buildings such as the steel works at Port Talbot or the power station at Didcot, because there are several places where the drawings of these buildings would be stored. In the case of Didcot power station, drawings would exist at the Central Electricity Generating Board, in the architect's office, the county planning office and possibly in the offices of the insurance company. Modern or twentieth-century buildings should all have drawings for their construction and working stored somewhere. The fourth factor is the enthusiasm of the team available to do the work of measurement; their ability to work together; and their mutual enjoyment of discovery and research. The fifth is the amount of time available, if a decision to demolish has already been taken.

A relatively small amount of equipment is required to measure a building successfully. A measuring tape either 30m (100 ft) or 15m (50 ft) long is essential. This should either be a steel ribbon tape or a cloth tape woven around longitudinal steel wires. For short and detailed measurements a 6-ft folding measuring rod is to be preferred to the flexible type. The reason for this is that the flexible tape has to be held at both ends, whereas the measuring rod can be poked across an opening and does not need to be held at both ends. The recording of notes, sketches and measurements can be done in two different ways. The author prefers a hard-backed book 10 in. by 8 in., or A4 or foolscap—with plain paper. In his view this is better than a board on which a loose pack of sheets of paper is held in place by a large 'bulldog' clip. The use of a hard-backed book means that the sheets are kept in sequence and, on a windy day, are protected by the cover when not in use.

The previous items are essential but the following are needed in some instances and can be taken to the site for use if required. A hammer and some 6-in. nails or short meat skewers should be taken if the industrial archaeologist is working on his own or with only one assistant. This enables the zero end of the measuring tape to be fixed at the start of a run of dimensions and then the tape can be run out from there to take the other dimensions. A stick of ordinary blackboard chalk should always be available, as this enables points of reference to be marked on a building as necessary. A ball of white string and some straight rods can also be useful in instances when buildings have irregular shapes. A torch should always be included for work in dark corners.

There are several rules for measuring buildings which are worth observing to ensure that a good level of accuracy can be maintained. Linear dimensions—along the wall of a factory for example—should be taken from a single point and each point for which a dimension is required should have its dimension referred to this single (zero) point. The reason for this is so that any errors of measurement are kept within each dimension. If each detail was measured separately then the errors would be added to each other over the whole length of the wall, thus producing a considerable cumulative error. With the first method the dimensions do not have to be added together to get the length of the wall so there is only one error possible. If there is a break in the wall, measure this from the zero point and then start again with a new zero at this point. When measuring the inside shape of a room or factory space, as many diagonals as possible should be taken. This will enable the shape to be plotted accurately by means of the triangles of dimensions which have been obtained. If a room is floored with sawn boards its squareness can sometimes be plotted by the way the boards run out against the wall. If a building is very irregular in shape, one way of measuring this irregularity is by creating a square or rectangular shape around the building with the string and straight rods. The string is set up parallel to one side, as far as possible, then the other sides are set up using 3:4:5 triangles at the corners. The author uses pieces of string 900mm (3 ft), 1200mm (4 ft) and 1500mm (5 ft) long to do this. When the shape has been completed around the building its dimensions are noted. Any prominent features on the walls are related to the string and to their positions on the walls. Then, using a pre-determined series of points on the strings —at 3m (10 ft) intervals, for example—the distance of the walls from these points on the strings is noted. When the drawing is begun, the string shape is put on the drawing paper in light pencil and the outline of the building

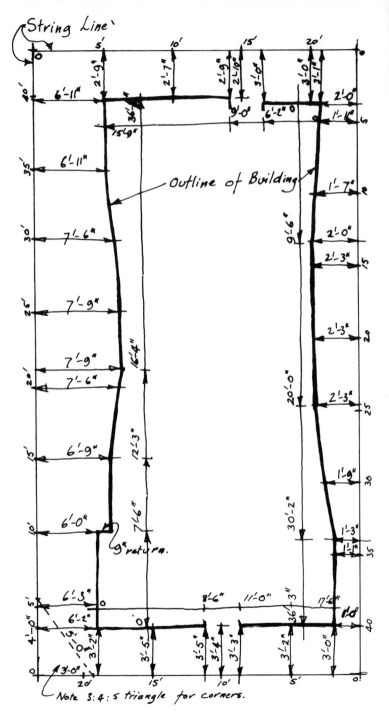

2 Diagram showing how an irregularly shaped building is measured by creating a rectangle outside it

plotted from there. Figure 2 shows this method. The plotting of external heights is difficult for one person to do but with two it is relatively easy. Place one person on top of the building, or as high as is practicable. Using the long tape with a weight (such as a bunch of keys) fastened on to the zero loop, the levels of the various elements of the façade can be read off by the person at the upper level against the point chosen as the zero—a window-sill or parapet would be suitable. From there, an upward reference to a window-head, eaves and gutter line can be added to the run of dimensions by means of a 6-ft rod. Figure 3 shows this. At the same time a reference can be made from the outside zero point to an inside run of dimensions by relating the zero point over the sill to the floor inside. When measuring inside a building, try to find a point at which a tape can be dropped right down the building: a stair-well, or, in a mill, a line of sack-traps, would be suitable. When measuring a roof, the slope can be determined inside by using a method of triangulation. A portion of the slope is measured. From the top point of this portion drop a plumb bob (string and keys) and from the bottom point measure horizontally to the string of the plumb bob.

Measuring machinery requires more skill but, once experience has been gained on buildings, the same rules apply to machines. However, there are certain added difficulties in terms of shapes when it comes to machinery. In the case of circles, small diameters can be measured with calipers. Larger diameters should be measured by holding two rods parallel to each other and touching the diameter of the object being measured; then measure the gap between the rods and this gives the diameter. Gearing is not easy to measure unless one is a qualified mechanical engineer. Edge-to-edge or spur gears are easier, for here the number of teeth and the distance between the centres of the wheels can be measured. Always count all the teeth in a gear wheel, marking the first in the count with chalk. Gear wheels frequently have 'hunting' teeth in their arrangement. These are odd teeth on one or other wheel which enable any unevenness in the gear cutting to be evened out. At each revolution of the wheels, the same teeth do not engage with each other. Bevel gears are harder to measure. The first point to remember about bevel gears is that the angle at which the gears meet is subtended by a point at which the centre lines of both shafts would meet. Teeth counts should be made and the size of the teeth noted. The dimensions of the rims carrying the teeth are important as they relate to the angle at which the bevel teeth meet.

The industrial archaeologist would clearly be daunted by the prospect of measuring and drawing a steam engine, gas engine or internal combustion engine. If he is not professionally involved with this type of machinery he should consult someone with the requisite knowledge. There is no point in preparing a measured drawing of an engine when drawings of it already exist and may even have been published. The work of recording is so vital that it would be wrong to spend time on duplicating an existing measured drawing. There must, however, be occasions when a piece of machinery is too old for there to be any drawings of it preserved. In such a case the industrial archaeologist should try to make his measurements relate the machine to the building in which it is housed. If the machine is on a bed plate then two sides of this should be related to the walls of the building. In Figure *16* this is demonstrated by the relation between the hurst frame and the adjacent walls. The industrial archaeologist should measure a machine in relation to his drawing requirements. Is it only to be part of the general arrangement drawings of a building or is it to be detailed on its own? The measurements of machinery for a drawing produced at a scale of 1:50 are very different and less detailed than those for a drawing of a machine at a scale of 1:10 or even 1:20. For the general arrangement drawing measurements should be made of overall details and not of particular points such as bolt sizes. However, the measurements of the inside of cylinders and cylinder stroke will be needed because these will be of assistance in the interpretation of the use of the building and the contribution made by the machine to an industrial process. The industrial archaeologist will make his measurements basically in the order of plan, section and elevation. However, for a large scale drawing of only a particular machine the industrial archaeologist may well have to dismantle parts to gain access to the inside of cylinders, to the piston rings or to other details. He may very sensibly measure and draw each of the various parts as they are exposed. Sketches in perspective or freehand isometric projection may be the best way to show each item and the part it plays in the whole machine.

It is clear that the industrial archaeologist will need assistance in the measuring of machinery and an engineer will be invaluable in helping him to understand the machine. Measuring a machine without the assistance of someone who knows how it was put together and how it works may lead the industrial archaeologist to make mistakes. If the machine has had to be measured without professional assistance it should also be photographed thoroughly. Before the drawings are put on the drawing board the material should be discussed with an engineer who can help with its interpretation. There are many points which an engineer would spot which might be overlooked by the industrial archaeologist. Given time the experienced fieldworker can make satisfactory measured drawings of machinery. The author knows an enthusiast who makes his own measured drawings of locomotives which he has measured in the scrap yard at Barry!

In the preparation of measured drawings the ideal is that someone else can pick up the measurement notes and prepare drawings from them. This is possible if a good series of photographs of the building has been taken to fill in the details. However, the industrial archaeologist will normally be so keen on a project that he will want to do his own measured drawings. When preparing the measurement sketches on site, the person who is going to do the actual finished drawings should be the person who does the sketches and adds the dimensions to them. At least, when he comes to a sticky point in translating the dimensions to the drawings, he can blame no one but himself for the unreadable or wrong dimension! A further point is that he will know the order of the dimensions he needs for the drawings he proposes to do. When three industrial archaeologists are able to work together, one should hold the zero end of the tape and the second should hold the tape box so that he can read off the running dimensions, whilst the third has the sketch and marks down the dimensions as they are read off. With two people the recorder should hold the zero end of the tape and the second person reads off the running dimensions. With only one person, the zero end has to be held on a nail and the recorder also reads off and marks down the running dimensions—sometimes a difficult process.

The equipment needed for preparing measured drawings consists of a drawing board and Tee-square, an adjustable set-square, a 30/60 set-square and a box of drawing instruments. For the beginner, the best type of drawing board is the old type of battened board with a loose Tee-square. The drawing machine with fixed parallel motion and fixed set-squares is a sophisticated instrument which, whilst excellent for the professional draughtsman, requires a great deal of experience to be used properly. The board should be covered with a backing sheet of cartridge or detail paper. Over this a sheet of tracing paper should be fixed with draughting tape— not with drawing pins. It is important that pin holes are not left in the middle of the board as this causes difficulties if compasses are used on the board at a later date. The compass has a fine, shouldered point, and it is awkward if this pierces the sheet into a larger pin hole.

The drawing should be made in black indian ink on tracing paper or tracing cloth. This enables many prints to be made of the drawing, either by photocopying or Xerox copying. The setting-out work should be done in pencil. The author uses an HB pencil, held very lightly, for all his work. The advantage is that, held lightly, it does not incise the surface of the sheet and it erases easily. It is important to use a light pencil so that it rubs out quickly and does not take away the ink when it is rubbed out. The pencil rubber should be a very soft one which does not reduce the density of the black ink line. The pen to use for inking-in can be the traditional draughtsman's ruling pen in which the ink is placed by a quill between the two nibs and adjusted in width by a screw. This older type of instrument was replaced after the Second World War by the 'Graphos', a fountain-pen version of the ruling pen. Shortly after the production of the 'Graphos', a stylus pen, the 'Rapidograph', was brought out and this has proved to be of wide use for all types of draughtsmanship. This pen has a series of nib sizes which produce lines of known thickness under all circumstances, provided they are held nearly vertically. They can be used for freehand drawing (which the ruling pen cannot), for ruling lines with the Tee-square and for stencil lettering. The only rule attached to using pens is to keep them clean and to empty them after each unit of work so that they do not dry hard between drawings. The best ink to use is the one marketed under the pen's trade name. If an ink line has gone wrong, it should be erased by a single-edged razor blade and not an ink rubber. The surface of the drawing can be got ready for more ink working by rubbing pencil into it and this is then taken off with a pencil rubber at the end of the work. Do not rub out the pencil lines except in one operation at the end. This prevents reducing the quality of the ink.

The normal type of drawing is an orthographic projection, also called a third-angle projection. Here the object, or building, is drawn in plan, elevation and end elevation. Figure 4 shows the horse wheel at Shabden Park in Surrey. This shows the building in plan and elevation. The end elevation has been replaced by a cross section since the elevations are basically all the same. The plan has been duplicated at roof level to show the various elements of roof construction and the slate-lined water tank held on the tie beams of the roof structure. Figures 20 to 26 show Dowrich Mill in Devon. This is a third-angle-projection set of drawings but they have been spread out over several sheets to make the overall sheet size smaller, thereby doing away with excessive folding of the drawings. This has a further value in that one sheet can be laid over the next, which saves time in setting up the drawing. Figures 5 to 7 show the only three sheets of drawings of the brewhouse of the Wellington Arms, Stratfield Turgis, Hampshire. The elevations were so plain that there was no point in drawing these; the important point was the disposition of the brewing equipment, tuns, coppers and fermenting vessels. Often machinery needs a considerable amount of explanation if one is to understand it properly. The isometric drawing is the best in these circumstances as it enables one to look right into the drawing and see the disposition of the parts and their relation-

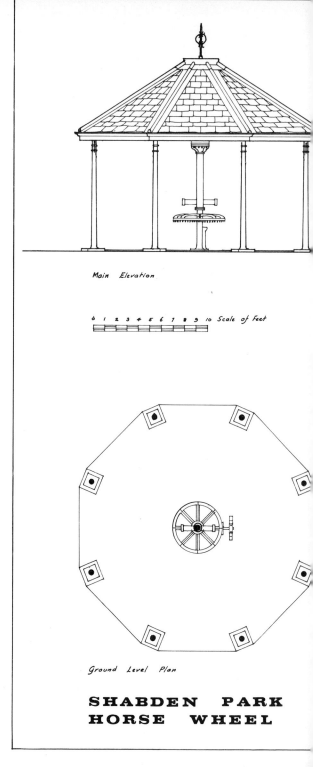

Main Elevation

0 1 2 3 4 5 6 7 8 9 10 Scale of Feet

Ground Level Plan

SHABDEN PARK
HORSE WHEEL

4   The horse wheel, Shabden Park, Surrey, which is to be re-erect

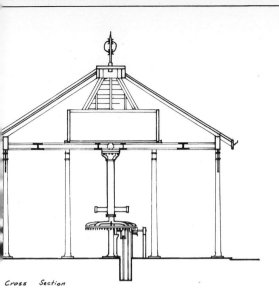

Cross   Section

0   1   2   3   4 Scale of Metres

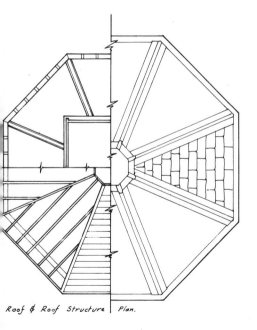

Roof & Roof Structure | Plan.

Measured Hugo Brunner & J. Kenneth Major
Drawn   J. Kenneth Major   October 1973.

Court, Henley-on-Thames

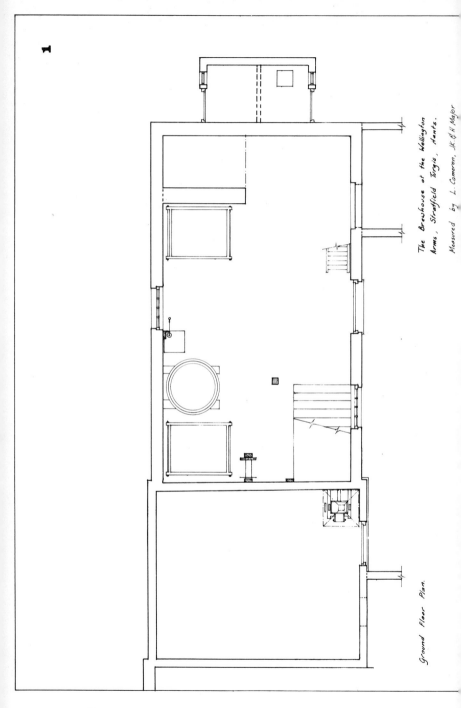

The Brewhouse at the Wellington Arms, Stratfield Turgis, Hants.

Measured by L. Cameron, JK & H. Major

Ground Floor Plan.

5   Measured drawing of ground floor plan of Wellington Arms brewhouse, Stratfield Turgis, Hampshire

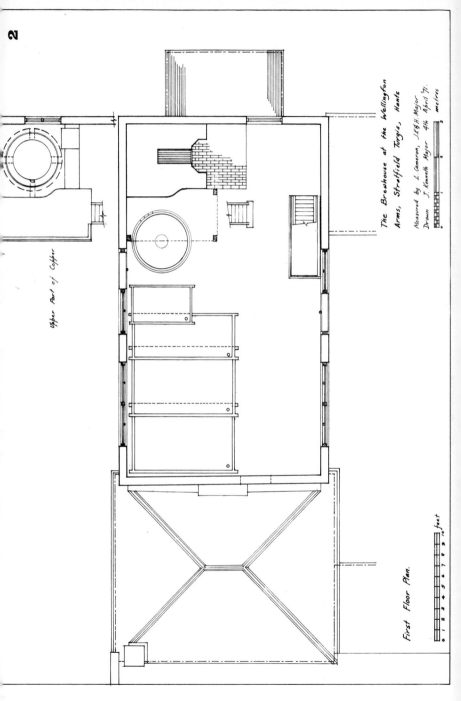

The Brewhouse at the Wellington Arms, Stratfield Turgis, Hants

Measured by L Cameron, J.E&H Major
Drawn J. Kenneth Major 4th April '71.

metres

Upper Part of Copper

First Floor Plan.

feet

6   Measured drawing of first floor plan of Wellington Arms brewhouse

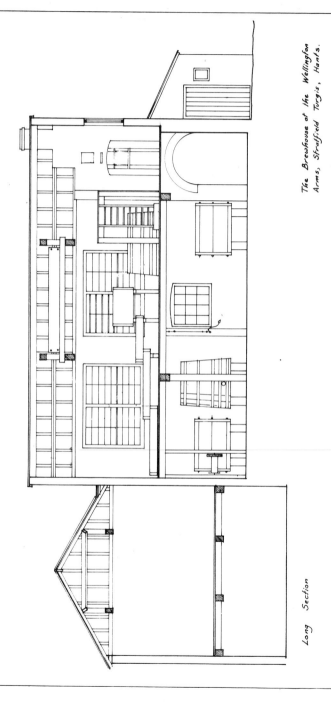

The Brewhouse of the Wellington Arms, Stratfield Turgis, Hants.

Measured by L. Cameron, J.K & H. Major
Drawn by J. Kenneth Major 4th April 71

Long Section

7 Measured drawing of the long section of Wellington Arms brewhouse

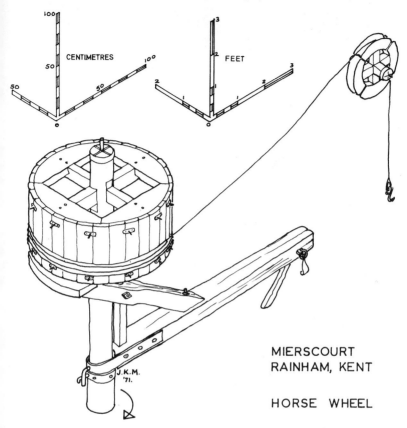

CENTIMETRES

FEET

MIERSCOURT
RAINHAM, KENT

HORSE WHEEL

J.K.M.
'71.

8   Isometric drawing of rope-winding horse wheel, Mierscourt, Rainham,
Kent

ship one to the other. Figure *8* shows the horse wheel at Mierscourt, Kent,
which raised water from a well by means of a bucket which was lifted by a
rope which was wound on to the large drum as the horse walked in a
clockwise direction. When the horse stopped, the horse arm dropped and
the brake came into contact with the drum and the clutch hook at the
bottom was disconnected. The structure of the little shed has been omitted
to show the machine in its entirety. Using the isometric projection the
items in the structure of the wheel are quite clear, and the working of the
brake and the clutch hook easily understood.

Lettering on drawings is very important. If one looks at existing books
which demonstrate the various aspects of industrial archaeology one is

aware of this importance. There are several mechanical forms of lettering which look neat. There are the 'Uno' and 'Standardgraph' stencils where a stylus pen traces out the letter. Then there is the stuck-on type of lettering of which 'Letraset' is an example. These letters are rubbed off the back of transparent film on to the sheet of tracing paper and then 'boned' into place with a ruler end. Freehand lettering needs a great deal of practice before one can be confident that one has an acceptable hand which can be used on published drawings. Lettering should always be consistent in type and size. A 'Guideline' stencil is useful to get parallel setting-out lines for hand lettering.

The example chosen to show how the measured drawings of an industrial building are tackled is a small watermill, called Dowrich Mill, which is situated on the river Creedy about six miles upstream from Crediton in Devon. In this instance, the author and his wife measured the building together in about eight hours. The investigation, photographs and report had been done on a previous visit by the author on his own and this had taken about six hours.

The following figures show exactly what each sheet of measurements contained. Unfortunately the field notes were written in pencil, so for the purposes of reproduction, each sheet has been traced, or re-drawn when a tracing would have been too large for the pages of this book. The pages of the field notebook are 10 in. by 8 in. so it is easy to see that there is not a great deal of reduction in size when these have had to be re-drawn. The measurements were supplemented by some 30 photographs of which five are reproduced here. These photographs show the mill in some detail and give the reader an idea of the relationship between the measurement and the building.

Plate 31 is a downstream view of the mill. The photograph was taken at a point on top of the presumed route of the underground tail-race. The reader will note how the more recent extension, built of clay lump and stone, is out of line with the original building. The waterwheel is just visible on the left wall of the original building. Embedded timber pieces can be seen in the clay-lump wall behind the sapling in the foreground. Plate 32 shows the side of the building opposite the wall where the water-wheel and gearing is mounted. In this picture the slope of the ground is apparent as well as the various door and window openings and the decay of the roof and structure. Plate 33 shows the extremely derelict waterwheel. The value of this picture is that it shows the construction of the wheel in considerable detail. The details of the cast-iron slots holding the buckets in place and of the overlapping joints between the rims can be clearly seen. The shapes of the cast-iron walls forming the sockets for the spokes

31   Dowrich Mill, Devon, downstream view

32   Dowrich Mill, view from mill yard

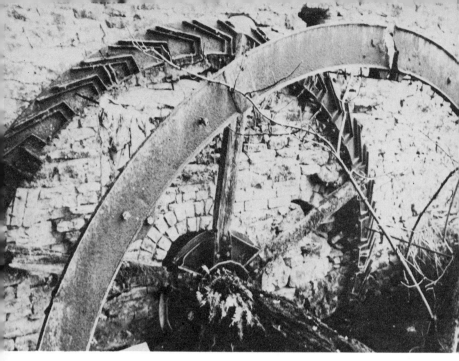

33 Dowrich Mill, derelict waterwheel

34 Dowrich Mill, gearing inside hurst frame

35   Dowrich Mill, area of first floor above hurst frame

on the hub boxes are also more clearly seen than would be the case on any drawing or sketch. Plate *34* shows the gear wheels inside the hurst frame. This particular hurst frame contains some fairly complicated geometry where the bridges overlap the main shaft or each other. The detail of the curves on the stops holding the bridge which carries the upright shaft can also be seen. Again, the detail of the tentering screw on the left post is shown clearly here. Plate *35* shows the first floor in the area above the hurst frame. Here the single lay shaft with its pulleys is visible, as well as the two pairs of millstones and the upright shaft. The wall behind the upright shaft shows the blocked window openings.

Figure *9* is the external outline of the ground floor. In view of the slope of the ground and the high wall at the top left of the drawing, some difficulty was experienced with this plan. A nail was driven into the corner on point *A*, the tape was hooked over this and stretched to point *B*. From this tape the three points of measurement were made. These were the kink in the wall and the inside and outside of the quoin which lay parallel to the tape at this point. The distance from the kink to the tape was also

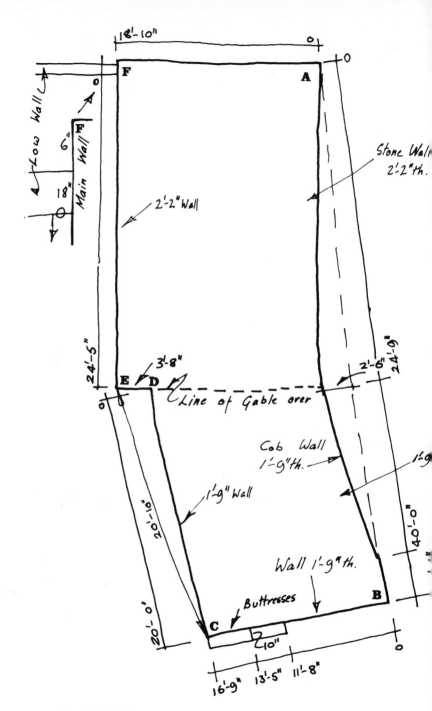

9 Dowrich Mill, Devon, measurement notes, sheet 1, external
dimensions of ground floor

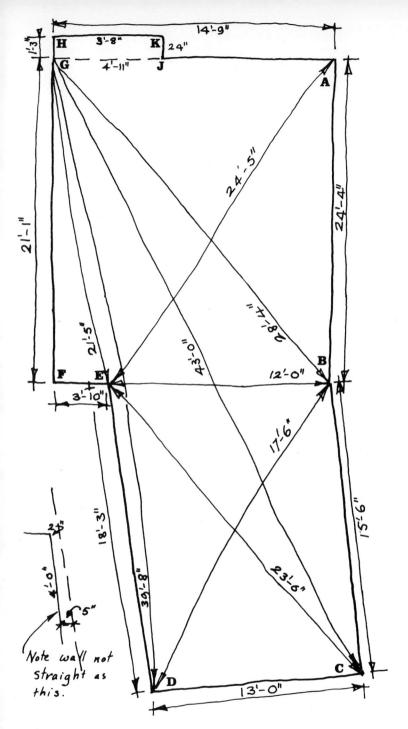

10 Dowrich Mill, measurement notes, sheet 2, internal dimensions of ground floor

measured. Wall BC was a straightforward wall to measure. Walls ED and DC were straight walls with only one measurement each. The diagonal EC was measured to enable the setting-out of the clay-lump wall to be determined. FE was measured at low level, and the setting-out of the wall and the zero point on the wall was measured at high level and added to the drawing. Figure *10* is the measurement of the inside of the ground floor. Each of the outside walls, AB, BC, CD, DE, EF, FG were dealt with as straight measurements. Point G was obtained by sighting AJ through to G, where a chalk mark was put on the wall. HKJG was measured with the measuring rod. This plan is important, because all the triangulation, setting out the building, was done at this stage. AG was chosen as the base of the triangle. Every possible triangle was measured so that AGFEB was plotted. A second series of triangles with the base EB was measured so that EBCD was plotted. The diagonal GD also showed up the irregularities in the clay-lump wall ED. This pair of sheets of sketches show how important it is to examine a building before actually setting out the proposed measurements.

Figure *11* shows the layout of the timbers forming the structure of the first floor. It has been drawn as though the first-floor boarding has been removed and one is looking down through it. Whilst the sizes have been indicated, these are in fact only the general sizes of the timbers; irregularities in the cutting make sizes differ considerably. The boards of this floor were generally 9 in. wide and were laid in accordance with the layout of the structural timbers below. Note how the same sizes can be indicated for a row of similar timbers.

Figure *12* is the first of the four elevations of the mill. This is the upstream elevation and was chosen as the starting elevation because it was used to fix a datum from which all the elevations could run. This datum was the horizontal portion of the verge boards. It was chosen because it related to the level of the slate eaves' line. The building also carried an Ordnance Survey broad arrow and this was also related to the chosen datum. By using a ladder the various dimensions were taken and the ground line was related to the datum. The lower portion of the drawing is of the window in the roof space. This was an old wooden-framed window which had been cut down to fit the opening. As the window had been built in the dead centre, no setting-out dimensions have been used. Figure *13* is the same as the elevation shown in Plate *32*. The eaves' line is the same line as the previously chosen datum and the building was low enough for that to be measured until the cob wall was reached. Here the dimensions were done by using the upper door. The door and window openings have been drawn with their frames, where these exist, but all the dimensions were taken of

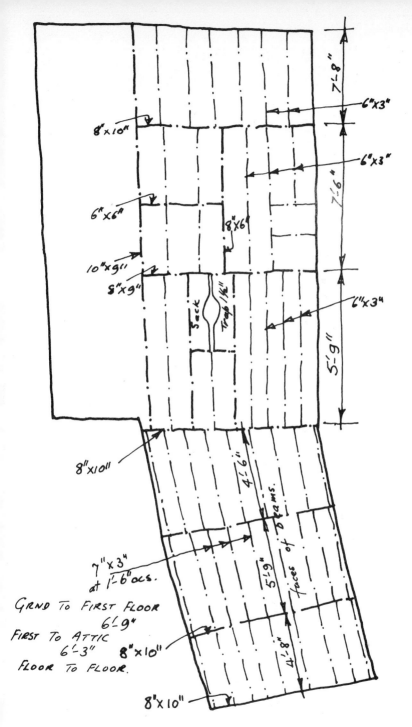

11 Dowrich Mill, measurement notes, sheet 3, floor structure of first floor

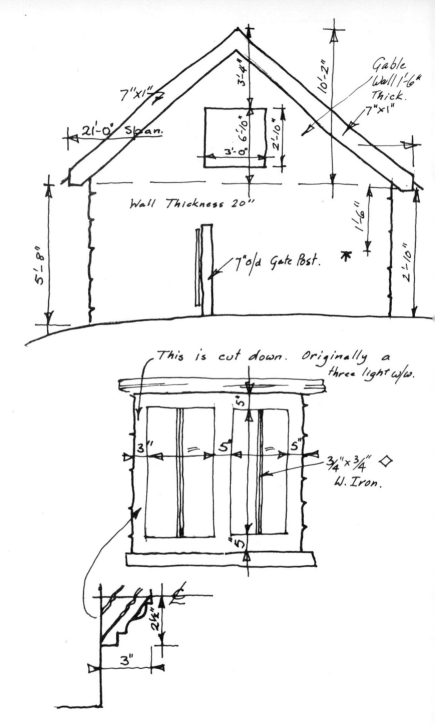

7"x1"

21'-0" Span.

3'-4"

10'-2"

Gable
Wall 1'-6"
Thick.
7"x1"

6'-0"

3'-0"

2'-10"

Wall Thickness 20"

1'-6"

5'-8"

7"o/d Gate Post.

2'-10"

This is cut down. Originally a
three light w/w.

5'

3"

5'

5"

3/4"x3/4" ◇
W. Iron.

5"

2½"

3"

12   Dowrich Mill, measurement notes, sheet 4, north elevation of mill

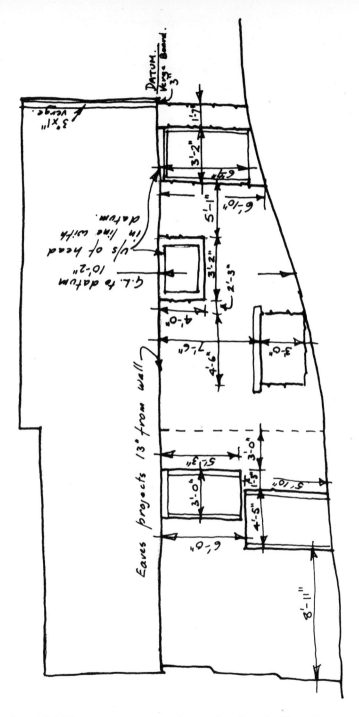

13   Dowrich Mill, measurement notes, sheet 5, elevation of mill on side
opposite waterwheel

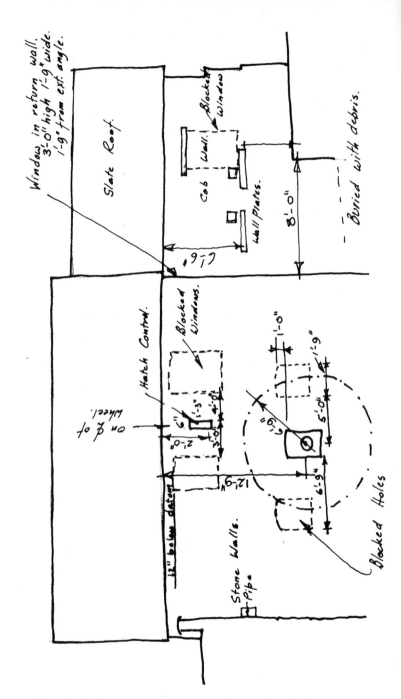

14 Dowrich Mill, measurement notes, sheet 6, elevation of side containing waterwheel

the structural openings. Figure *14* is of the wall on which the waterwheel is mounted. Note how the walls have not been given a true depth because the overlying debris was not removed before the measurements were taken. The eaves' line is again the datum. Where old openings existed in this wall they have been drawn on and measurements given. This is important because these openings relate to an earlier arrangement of the mill gearing. The various wall plates have been added to the drawing of the cob wall. The waterwheel is shown but the centre line of the shaft is not dimensioned on this drawing as it is detailed on the hurst-frame drawing. Figure *15* of the downstream elevation is quite straightforward.

Figure *16* is the plan at ground level of the hurst frame. Using the same reference points as those on the inside plan of the ground floor (Fig. *9*), the various elements of the hurst frame are dimensioned. The double post at point X caused some difficulty as it made the triangle XZG awkward to measure. One way to clear this is to measure the post which is in the way and then measure from the face of the post to Z or G and add the dimensions of the post. Similarly the triangle FWY is dimensioned. Here you will notice a discrepancy of an inch in WY: the inside dimension of the pit is 4 ft 7 in., the overall dimension WY is 5 ft 3 in., leaving 8 in. for the horizontal width of the baulk of timber forming the sill, which in fact measured 9 in. by 6 in. A discrepancy of one inch in a rough-hewn stone wall or timber baulk is not an error about which one should be worried. The reader will notice that this drawing gives a new datum which is the top of the timber sill and also the centre line of the main shaft. This enables the internal datum and the external datum to be related to each other. The various walls of the wheel pit and of a long depression stretching the whole length of the 'wheel' wall are visible. Subsequent excavation has shown this depression to be an earlier wheel pit. Figure *17* is the elevation of the hurst frame on the line YZ but taken through the two floors. The first point to note is that the vertical dimensions have been omitted as these were noted on the plan (Fig. *11*). This drawing is important because it gives the sizes of the various items of gearing and their relative positions. This drawing is one which needs the amplification of the detailed photographs. The position of the bridges is of particular importance. Timber baulks WY and XZ are permanently mounted and in their turn carry the timber bridge UV which supports the upright shaft. Two further hinged bridges on lines WY and XZ project through the outer posts at Y and Z where they are supported by adjustable screws. These bridges (tentering bridges) support the stone spindles and the upper stone of each pair of millstones.

Figure *18* is the drawing which gives the details of the waterwheel and

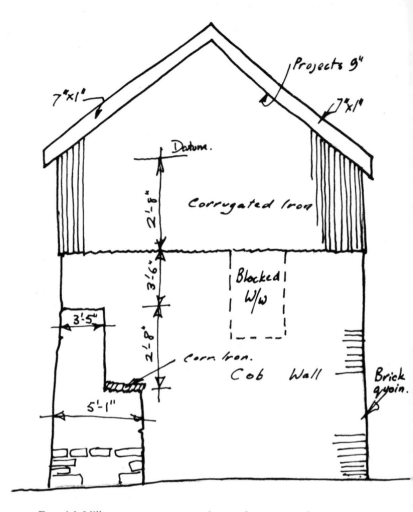

Projects 9"

7"x1"

7"x1"

Datum.

2'-6"

Corrugated Iron

3'-6"

Blocked
W/w

3'-5"

2'-8"

Corr. Iron.

Cob   Wall

Brick
quoin.

5'-1"

15   Dowrich Mill, measurement notes, sheet 7, downstream elevation

also needs amplification by photographs. This is a situation in which an industrial archaeologist could carry a circle template so that he can get circles which look like circles on his notebook. The right-hand section of the drawing shows the relationship between the rims and spokes, hubs and main shaft. Note how the diminishing sections of the spokes are picked out. The details of the hub casting on the left has its basic dimensions on it—the thickness and diameter. The finer details are picked out from the photographs and added to the drawings. Similarly the detail of the rim is drawn in the top left-hand corner. What was important was the relation-

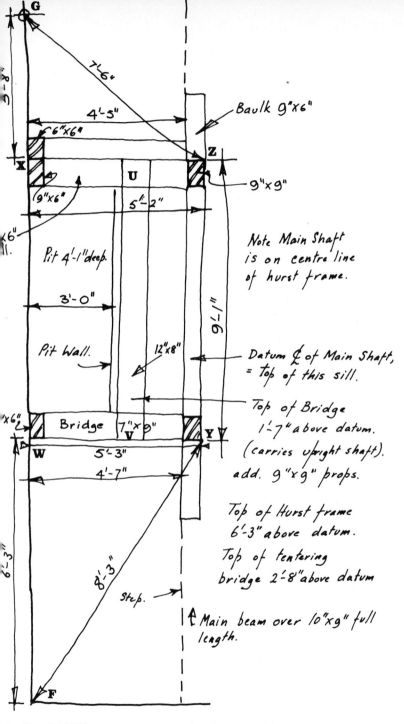

G

7'-6"

4'-5"

6"x6"

Baulk 9"x6"

Z

9"x9"

X

U

9"x6"

5'-2"

6"

Note Main Shaft
is on centre line
of hurst frame.

Pit 4'-1"deep.

3'-0"

9'-1"

Pit Wall.

12"x8"

Datum ℄ of Main Shaft,
= Top of this sill.

Top of Bridge
1'-7" above datum.
(carries upright shaft).
add. 9"x9" props.

6"

Bridge 7"x9"

V

Y

W

5'-3"

4'-7"

Top of Hurst frame
6'-3" above datum.

Top of tentering
bridge 2'-8"above datum

6'-3"

8'-3"

Step.

℄ Main beam over 10"x9" full
length.

F

16   Dowrich Mill, measurement notes, sheet 8, setting of hurst frame on
ground floor

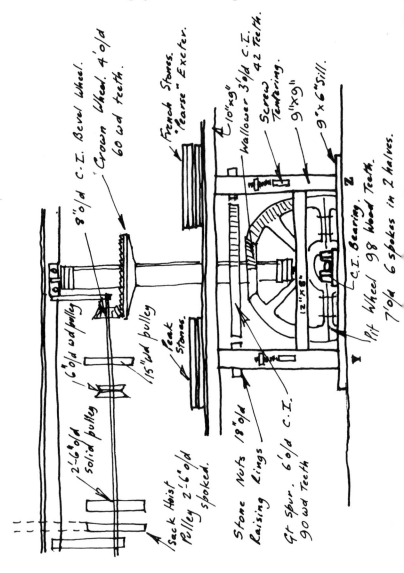

17   Dowrich Mill, measurement notes, sheet 9, details of gearing and machinery

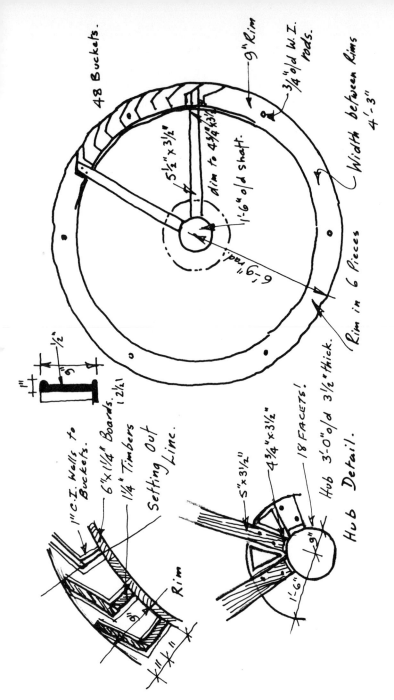

48 Buckets.

9" Rim

3/4" o/d W.I. rods.

Width between Rims 4'-3"

5½" x 3½"

Rim to 4¾"x3½"

1'-6" o/d shaft.

6'-9" rad.

Rim in 6 Pieces

1" C.I. Walls to Buckets.

6"x1¼" Boards.

1¼" Timbers 1 2½"1

Setting Out Line.

Rim

6"

9"

11"x4"

5"x3½"

4¾"x3½"

18 FACETS!

Hub 3'-0" o/d 3½" thick.

Hub Detail.

9"

1'-6"

½"

6"

1"

18   Dowrich Mill, measurement notes, sheet 10, details of waterwheel

ship between the outer edge of the bucket and the radial bottom-board of the bucket. The cross section of the rim is drawn heavily and this drawing shows the wall thicknesses of the casting and the walls supporting the buckets.

Figure *19* shows the two cross sections of the roof structure, the main building and the extension. The first point to note is that the slope of the roof has not been added to this drawing. The slope was accurately—and more easily—measured on the elevation shown in Figure *12*. Only half of each section is drawn, a fact which is shown by the presence of the centre line, marked *CL*. The sections of the timber principals are measured—again because of rough timbers—and these have been taken as a mean size. In this instance the slating battens have not been measured as they were extremely variable and are spaced at reducing centres to match the courses of the slates on the roof.

Measurement sketches like these, together with the representative and detailed photographs, are the basis on which the seven sheets of finished drawings were produced. In view of the very rough—and somewhat decayed—character of the mill, the author adopted his usual style of freehand drawing. The basic dimensions were all drawn on the sheets of tracing paper in light pencil and then the freehand, working with 'Rapidograph' stylus pens nos 2 and 4, was done over the pencil work.

Figure *20* (sheet *1* of the set of 7) shows the ground-floor plan of the mill and the surroundings. In theory this is a section taken about 5 ft above ground level so that all the openings are properly shown. This section has been varied at certain places to make a more valid drawing. In the case of the waterwheel, this is just above the shaft so that the whole cross section of the wheel is shown. The inside of the hurst frame is shown with a section line just below the wallower and this enables the bridge supporting the upright shaft to be shown. No details have been added to the floor as it lay under a thick layer of manure. The pit had been excavated and so its details were known. Figure *21* (sheet 2) shows the first floor. The section line of the walls has been taken at a level which shows the two windows and the two doors. The whole of the gearing on this floor has been shown by assuming that the section line was above it in that area. This slight falsification is deliberate as it gives point to the gearing layout in full. At this level the whole of the waterwheel is visible in plan. The author chose to draw all the buckets in place, though none was present. To do this gives more point to the drawing. However, he was unable to draw the launder accurately and this is in position by a dotted line. A further item to note is the difference between the two pairs of millstones. The pair on the left is a pair of French stones, with balance boxes set into the rims, whilst

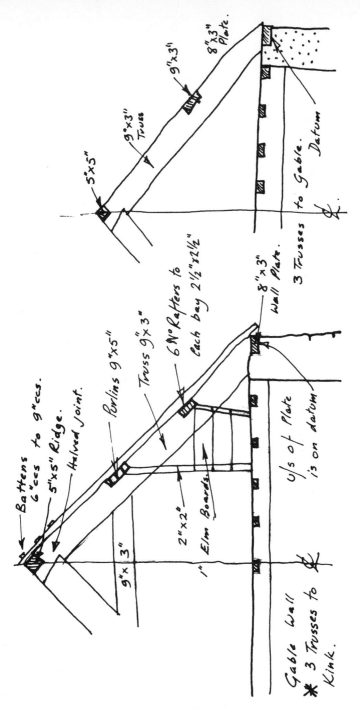

19   Dowrich Mill, measurement notes, sheet 11, roof cross sections

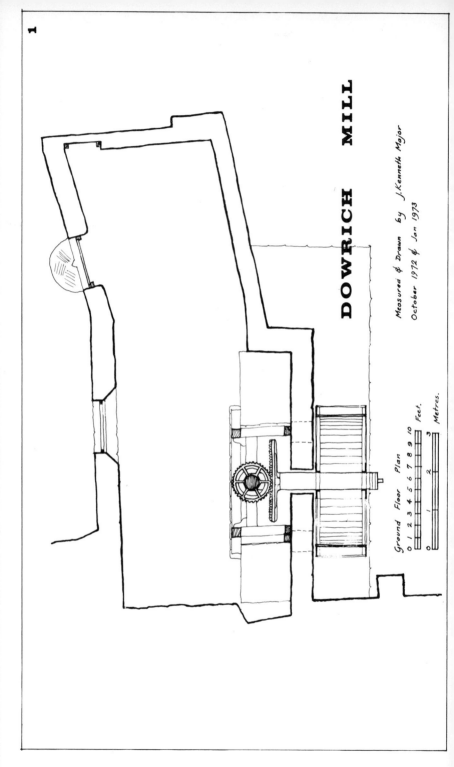

DOWRICH MILL

Measured & Drawn by J. Kenneth Major

October 1972 & Jan 1973

Ground Floor Plan

0 1 2 3 4 5 6 7 8 9 10 Feet.

0 1 2 3 Metres.

20 Dowrich Mill, finished measured drawings, sheet 1, ground floor plan

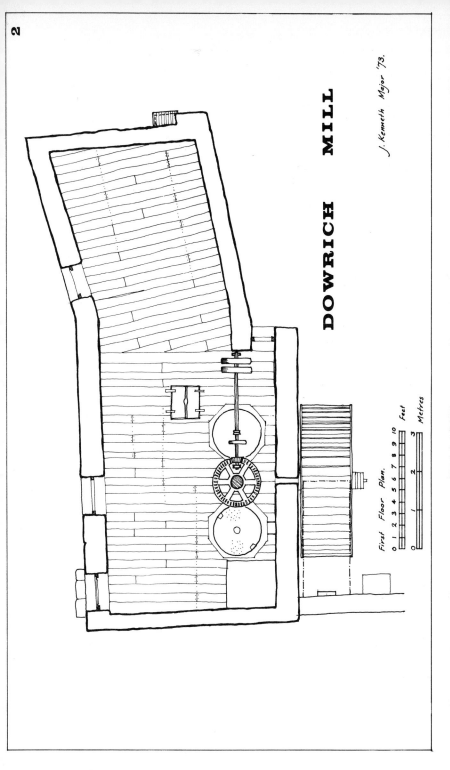

DOWRICH MILL

J. Kenneth Major '73.

First Floor Plan.

0 1 2 3 4 5 6 7 8 9 10 Feet

0 1 2 3 Metres

21   Dowrich Mill, finished measured drawings, sheet 2, first floor plan

the pair on the right are of millstone grit. Though no plan has been drawn of the structure of the first floor, the floor boards have been set out as the grid of structural timbers underneath was known.

Figure 22 (sheet 3) is the first of the three sheets of elevations and is chosen because the waterwheel makes it the most important of the four elevations. Note that the drawing distinguishes between the clay-lump walls and the stone areas of wall. However, in drawing stones, care must be taken to ensure that they are correctly to scale. This must be measured on site by measuring the size of the stones up a quoin and then running the courses in from that. When the slates were drawn in, the coursing was determined from a photograph. The blocked window openings have been drawn on this elevation because, in the view of the author, these were important to the understanding of the building. Figure 23 (sheet 4) shows the elevation of the mill facing the mill yard. As with sheet 3, the difference between brick, stone and clay lump has been drawn. Note the heads of the windows and doors indicated as timber. Here the indication of grain is diagrammatic rather than representational. The wheel mounted on this wall has subsequently proved to have no significance to the mill or its millwork. Figure 24 (sheet 5) shows the two short elevations of the mill. The upstream elevation contains the old timber window frame. Note the Ordnance Survey mark correctly positioned. This gives the level of the mill in relation to the river and would be important in studying the relationship of the waterwheel to the weir and river. The downstream elevation shows the extension and its skew setting-out in relation to the gable wall of the original mill. On this elevation, the difference between corrugated-iron sheets, clay lump and stone has been indicated. In both cases, the near elevation has been drawn in firmly with the differences in distance indicated but the further parts have been drawn in lightly with no detail shown. The waterwheel has again been reproduced with its buckets but the bearings have not been drawn because they were missing.

Figures 25 and 26 (sheets 6 and 7) show the long and cross sections of the mill. Perhaps these are the most important drawings because they show the disposition of the gearing and the structure which supports it. In the mill the gearing and floor have slipped but in the drawing this has been straightened up. This is a very conventional layout of gearing, so there is no need to supplement the drawing with a further drawing of the gearing in isometric projection. The cross section through the waterwheel was added because it was felt to be a valuable record of the construction of this important element of the millwork. It has also proved useful to provide a balanced sheet of drawings.

It should be explained that the reason for this number of sheets has

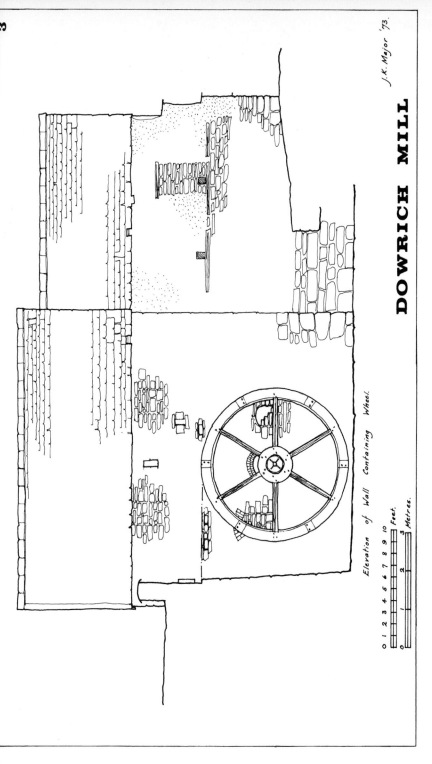

DOWRICH MILL

J. K. Major '73.

Elevation of Wall Containing Wheel.

0 1 2 3 4 5 6 7 8 9 10 Feet.

0 1 2 3 Metres.

22 Dowrich Mill, finished measured drawings, sheet 3, elevation of wall
containing waterwheel

Elevation to Mill Yard.

0 1 2 3 4 5 6 7 8 9 10 Feet.

0 1 2 3 Metres.

23 Dowrich Mill, finished measured drawings, sheet 4, elevation to mill yard

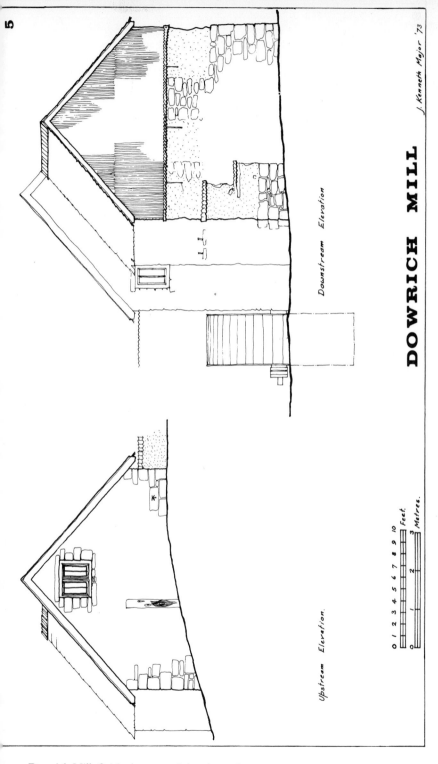

DOWRICH MILL

J. Kenneth Major '73

Downstream Elevation

Upstream Elevation.

0 1 2 3 4 5 6 7 8 9 10 Feet.

0 1 2 3 Metres.

24 Dowrich Mill, finished measured drawings, sheet 5, upstream and downstream elevations

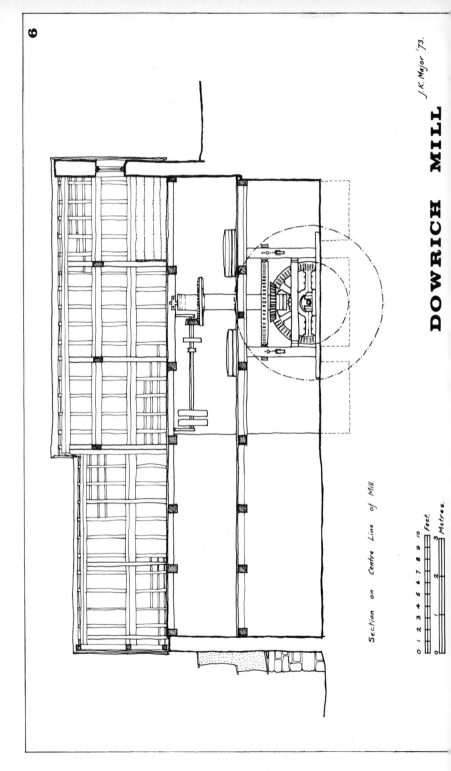

J. K. Major '73.

Section on Centre Line of Mill.

0 1 2 3 4 5 6 7 8 9 10 Feet.
0 1 2 3 Metres.

25   Dowrich Mill, finished measured drawings, sheet 6, section on centre line of mill

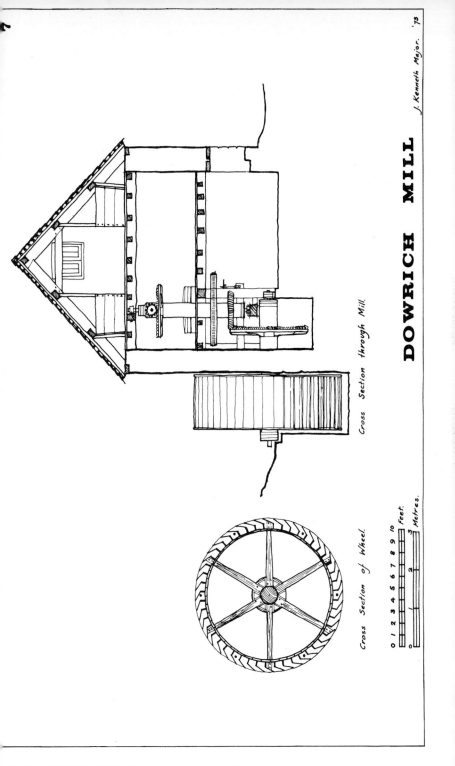

J. Kenneth Major. '75

Cross Section through Mill.

Cross Section of Wheel.

0 1 2 3 4 5 6 7 8 9 10 Feet.

0 1 2 3 Metres.

26   Dowrich Mill, finished measured drawings, sheet 7, cross sections
of the mill and waterwheel

been dictated by expediency. Each sheet can be left on the drawing board and the next laid over it. This saves time if the common setting-out lines are reproduced. In the case of the two opposite elevations, the first is turned over to give the setting-out lines of the second.

What standard should the industrial archaeologist seek to achieve when he completes his measured drawings? In the author's view, there are three books which show what can be achieved in the long term after years of practice. One, which is not all the work of professionals, is the *Report on Watermills Vol. 3 Scale Drawings*, published by Anders Jespersen in 1957. The second, which is the work of an architect, is *Windmills and Watermills*, by John Reynolds and published by Evelyn in 1970. The most recent is *A Report of the Mohawk–Hudson Area Survey*, published by the Smithsonian Institute in 1973. This volume represents the full-time hard labour of a group of student architects, historians and photographers. It was prepared with a great deal of planning so that a programme of measuring, photography and research work was put in hand. The drawings are very fine, if rather mechanical, but, bear in mind that these were very much 'rescue'

36   Bellamarsh Mill, Devon, measured and drawn by Bruce Bolton of Chudleigh

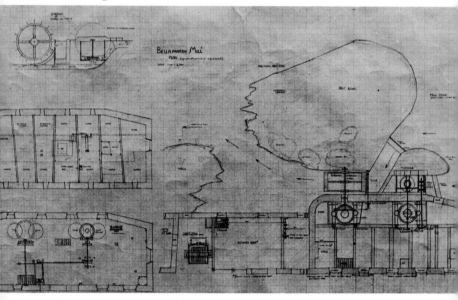

drawings, were produced for record purposes and are held in photographic archives.

Plate *36* shows a sheet of drawings of Bellamarsh Mill in Devon, which has been demolished. The author of these drawings, Bruce Bolton of Chudleigh, did the drawings before taking out the gearing in order to install it in another mill near Chudleigh. The drawings are a very good statement of the layout of the mill; they are plans together with a section through the double wheel space. Bruce Bolton chose to use squared paper with inch squares divided into 12, the side of each square representing 4 ft. The value of the drawings lies not in the finished quality of the drawings which, because of inexperience, were not intended for reproduction but in the valuable statements which they make about how Bellamarsh Mill worked; how the turbine had been inserted in the wheel space; and how the millstones were related to the waterwheels. The book, *Brindley at West Earth Colliery*, by Banks and Schofield, published by David and Charles in 1968, has good drawings based on fieldwork. These drawings are neatly lettered in a freehand style and are clear and uncluttered. The aim here was to interpret finds made in the peculiar hydraulic arrangements at the colliery. The drawings have done this and nothing has been added which could not be substantiated by evidence or knowledge.

Measured drawings should aim to supply knowledge of industrial monuments, what they looked like, what they were built of, and how the machinery in them was used. The industrial archaeologist should, therefore, give a neat statement of the building. This should be able to be reproduced so that it can be deposited in the right archives, or be published in a book or pamphlet or local-society journal.

6. Photography for the industrial archaeologist

The camera is the most important instrument which the industrial archaeologist takes with him when he goes out into the field. There are many occasions when he is not engaged in serious study but still wants his camera to make a record of something he has found and, whilst on holiday, he may find an industrial building being demolished which he knows is important enough to be recorded there and then.

Many people would claim that the standard of photography required by the various authorities as a record is beyond them and that they cannot compete with the professional photographer. The professional photographer has a completely different set of criteria which rule his finished photograph. If a particular piece of work being done by the industrial archaeologist requires a magnificent photograph, as for instance for an advertisement or in a series for a magazine article in which the illustrations are all important, then a professional could be used. The purpose of this chapter is to enable the industrial archaeologist to take adequate photographs for not only record purposes but also for publication when that is envisaged.

The photographer should always take his photographs with the highest standards in view. He might not think a monument important, but others may, and as a result he might have to publish his photographs in an article or book.

What type of photographs are required? The first clear need is for black-and-white photographs. The reason for this is that black-and-white negative material lasts very well for a long time if it is given the right treatment. Many copies can be made quite cheaply and selective enlargements are possible from small areas of the negative. Colour-negative stock and colour prints cannot be relied on to hold their colours indefinitely as the dyes are fugitive in the light and the material will lose colour and definition with age. Again other authorities who will want to make copy negatives or prints can only make them properly from black-and-white stock. These authorities are offices such as the National Monuments Record and the local record offices.

Very early in the industrial archaeologist's experience he will realize the importance of colour slides as a supplement to the black-and-white photographs he is taking. Frequently when attending conferences or lecture evenings there is an opportunity for members to show a few slides of a particular subject or interest. Later still in his experience the industrial archaeologist will be called upon to lecture about his particular subject or his discoveries in a chosen field and for this a collection of slides is essential. Industrial archaeology is essentially a subject requiring illustration and photographs and coloured slides are the means of giving this.

A point which concerns most industrial archaeologists is the cost of photography. People looking at photographic magazines are faced with a large range of expensive cameras. If the industrial archaeologist is coming to photography because of his interest in his subject, he should start with cameras and equipment of a modest type and he will find that he does not need to progress to complicated cameras, which are therefore expensive, until he has become very much more experienced.

The types of cameras which are best for the beginner are twin-lens reflex cameras, 35-mm range-finder cameras, and 35-mm single-lens reflex cameras. In terms of useful publishable photographs, the negative size should not be less than that of the conventional 35-mm camera, which has a negative size of some 25-mm vertically by 35-mm long. There are many excellent sub-miniature cameras on the market but their limitations really prevent their use by the dedicated industrial archaeologist. The twin-lens reflex is typified by the Rolleiflex or Rolleicord. Here a negative size of 6cm by 6cm or 4cm by 4cm and film with a backing paper is used. The camera is tall and the upper half contains a simple lens, which, by means of a mirror, produces a negative-size image on a screen inside a hood on top of the camera. The lower half contains the camera lens which projects its image on to the film at the back of the camera. The advantage of this camera lies in the excellence of the focus arrangements in the top mirror using the upper lens and in the size of the negatives produced. The principal disadvantage lies in the inability of the camera to take interchangeable lenses unless it is an extremely expensive model. The range-finder camera is typified by the Leica 35-mm camera but the more recent models are outside the means of most industrial archaeologists. In this type of camera the lens is coupled to a range-finder so that, in the manner of a conventional range-finder, the movement of the lens in and out adjusts the images in the range-finder and when these images overlap they are 'spot on' and the main lens is in focus. This is an extremely accurate type of camera and it can take various interchangeable lenses. The single-lens reflex 35-mm camera is the most popular of all the cameras on the market today. In this type of camera the image, again negative size, is produced on a screen by means of mirrors so that it can be looked at directly from above, like the Rolleiflex, or from behind through a pentaprism. When the exposure is made, the mirror moves out of the way and the opening shutter then exposes the film.

The industrial archaeologist should try to have a camera which gives a reasonable series of exposure periods and some slow speeds as well as the time exposure 'T' and the bulb exposure 'B'. Frequently the industrial archaeologist requires a camera to work in dark areas, in which case long exposures are needed. Long exposures mean that the camera has to be held steady and the best means of doing this is to use a tripod and to fire the camera's shutter by means of a flexible cable release. The camera should not be hand-held at speeds slower than 1/50th of a second, as the slightest tremor will produce a fuzzy out-of-focus enlargement. This should not prove a burden; the camera fixed on its tripod can be carried around any industrial monument complete.

Each film carries an exposure chart in its box and using this will enable the beginner to get an accurate speed setting—a certain speed with a certain stop. The stop is marked on the lens and refers to the width of the aperture inside the lens, expressed in relation to the focal length of the lens. The higher the stop number the better the definition over a greater distance. In industrial archaeology this is often an essential condition. The inside of an engine house, if photographed from one end, will have machinery in the near foreground as well as at the far end of the room and a photograph would need to be in focus from the foreground to the background. Use of a small stop—one with a high number—will produce this: f16 is a commonly used stop. Many lenses now have the depth of field marked on them so that the range of good focus is readily obtained.

When more experience has been gained, the industrial archaeologist will realize that he needs to use greater accuracy in setting the length of an exposure, particularly if he is working inside a building. The best way of determining an exposure is to use an exposure meter. It is better to have an exposure meter separate from the one mounted on the camera and connected to the shutter. Many situations require the photographer to make an average and this is not necessarily done correctly by using a meter on the camera. Further, if the industrial archaeologist is using two cameras, then he has the expense of only one exposure meter. The best-known make is the Weston Master. The cell receiving the light is approximately 2 in. in diameter. In dark situations the cell is uncovered and in open situations the cell is covered with a perforated screen. The reading is transferred from the moving needle to the dial where the reading translates into a relation between the required speed and the appropriate stop setting.

In considering the exposure, the alternative to the slow tripod shot is the flash gun and there are now two basic types of flash gun. The first is the battery-powered gun which uses flash bulbs. These are burnt out and thrown away after each shot. The second type is an electronic flash gun, in which a gas filled tube is fired as often as the subject demands. This gun is either battery-powered or mains-powered. The charge takes a few seconds to come up to strength (a small neon tube shows the state of readiness) and then the exposure is made. The gun has to recharge itself after each exposure. The great disadvantage of the flash gun is that it is mounted adjacent to the camera and therefore the result of the exposure is flat and lifeless because of the absence of shadows. The advantage of the medium size of electronic flash gun is the economy, as opposed to the expense of flash bulbs.

Every camera has a standard lens which is usually 5-cm focal length. The industrial archaeologist will quickly realize the inadequacy of this lens. When photographing interiors with this lens it will often not be possible to step back far enough to get everything into the frame. To enable this to be done a wide-angle lens will be necessary. If the wide-angle lens is 30- or 35-mm focal length there will be very little distortion; wider angles than this may produce an unacceptable distortion. If the industrial archaeologist wishes to photograph details at a distance, a telephoto lens is required. The generally accepted 135-mm length is the best for this work. A longer focal length would be unnecessary and needlessly expensive.

The industrial archaeologist will often wish to photograph objects close up. Details, cog wheels, 'finds' and drawings often need to be photographed in this way. Using the tripod again, the lens can be supplemented by a single lens which is screwed or fixed with a bayonet fitting on the front of the standard lens. Without alteration of the exposure the camera can get close to the item to be photographed and, with a 5-cm lens, a postcard can be reproduced on a standard 35-mm negative. If greater magnification is required, the lens can be brought further forward from the film. This is done by the insertion of extension pieces fixed between the lens and the camera body. Extension tubes must be used with care because the exposure must be adjusted according to a series of constants supplied with the extension pieces.

The industrial archaeologist will need a few more items of equipment which will make his photography more efficient and useful. He should always have a piece of chalk in his camera bag so that he can whiten letters on cast iron or mark in defective lettering on inscriptions. He should also have a scale stick—a stick with sections painted in inches and feet in alternate segments of black and white or red and white. A stout holdall to carry the equipment is important. Bearing in mind the sort of situations to be visited, the holdall should be workmanlike rather than luxurious.

The basic photographs produced by the industrial archaeologist are record photographs. These are plain statements of the facts of an industrial monument, as opposed to fine art studies, but that does not mean that care should not be taken. A few simple 'do's' and 'don't' are set out below as hints for producing a better quality picture. In the 'dont's' the following should be strictly adhered to:

(1)   Unless working at a speed of 1/50th of a second or faster, the camera should be tripod-mounted and not hand-held.
(2)   The camera should be held level and parallel to the horizon. The plane of the film in the camera should be vertical. The camera should not be tilted to get a whole building into the picture. If it is tilted then the vertical lines of the building will converge on the negative.
(3)   The camera should not point in the direction of the light source as this causes flare and halation on the negative.

Perhaps the 'do's' will be of more use as a guide to how to go about taking a photograph. In the correct order of action these are:

(a)   Load the camera in a dark corner out of direct light with a medium-speed film. In the case of a black-and-white film a speed of 125 ASA is suitable, or for colour 50 ASA.
(b)   If outside on a sunny day using black-and-white film add a yellow (2 times) filter to the lens.
(c)   Make sure that the object to be photographed is going to be adequately lit and avoid a really strong contrast between dark and light.
(d)   Having previously set your film speed on the exposure meter, take a reading of the subject. Try to avoid an unbalanced reading such as that which occurs when too much sky light is taken into the meter. Try to take an average reading for the subject which takes into account the various factors of the depth of shadow and the strongly lit areas.
(e)   Set the time of exposure and the aperture of the lens on the camera. This will be read from the exposure meter and transferred to the camera. However, it may well be that a particular speed is required, perhaps because of the movement of the subject or because the camera must be hand-held and this will determine the aperture automatically. Some subjects, however, require a greater depth of field and this will impose a small aperture of the lens, which in turn will lengthen the exposure.
(f)   Focus the camera. When the camera is being set to the correct focus,

care should be taken to focus on an object which will give the best depth of field in front of and behind that object.

(g)   Make the exposure using a firm stance and holding the camera in accordance with its shape and as suggested in its instruction booklet.

(h)   Wind on the film. You do not know how quickly your next exposure will be required and with some cameras the shutter is not locked by the film wind. Only by training yourself to wind on will you avoid two shots on one frame of the negative.

Before actually working with a camera in the field, the industrial archaeologist should practice with his camera so that he is wholly familiar with its working. When he starts work on an industrial monument he may not have the chance to go back to take any photographs which have not come out properly and must therefore be experienced in the use of his instruments.

Copying is an important aspect of photography for the industrial archaeologist and is described here although it is not part of his fieldwork

37   Method of copying small objects or documents using a tripod

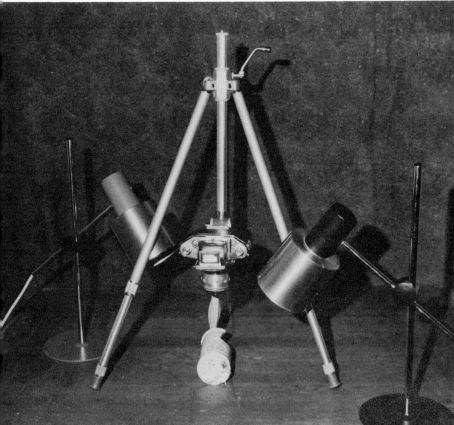

38 Trademark from a cream pot which is the object being photographed in Plate *37*

39 Domestic earthenware dug up on Marylebone Goods Yard

but an extension of it. Copying can be done quite easily with a minimum of equipment and the result will satisfy most of the requirements of the industrial archaeologist.

If the document to be copied is a large map or plan, a simple method is to pin it to a wall out of doors which faces north so that direct sunlight does not fall upon it. Then set up the camera so that it is centred on the map or plan and is parallel with its plane. The correct exposure at the smallest stop (or aperture) is set after an exposure meter has been consulted. The exposure is then made using a cable release.

Plate 37 shows a more complicated copying arrangement suitable for copying small objects or small documents such as postcards. A tripod having a reversible column is used and the camera is then mounted parallel to the base board or table. 'Proxar' lenses or extension tubes are added to the standard camera lens. Two identical table lamps are then placed on opposite sides of the object to be photographed and, by measurement, are set equidistant from the centre of the object. Then, after taking an exposure-meter reading, the exposure is made using a cable release to fire the shutter. Plate 38 shows the fine trademark from a small pot in which cream was delivered. The focus was such that the crackle in the glaze is visible.

Often objects or finds have to be photographed. Plate 39 shows a range of domestic earthenware dug up on the Marylebone Goods Yards during building operations following its closure. This is pottery which dates from before 1893, a date which is certain as that was the date when the compulsory purchase order was put in hand so that the railway could be built. The numbers are 'Letraset' numbers mounted on white card and the scale stick is marked in inches. The numbers enable the pots to be referred to in a description of the plate and the scale stick enables sizes to be determined.

Photography is a necessary skill for the industrial archaeologist. With care and experience a good result can be achieved which will satisfy most of his requirements.

7. Tools for the industrial archaeologist

The tools and clothing used by the industrial archaeologist in the field will depend to a large extent on the form of transport he has available. The author uses a motor-scooter and so he cannot be as well equipped as would be the case if he was using a car or van. The industrial archaeologist relying on public transport must be even more poorly equipped. However, many sites are out of the reach of mechanized transport and in these cases equipment must be reduced to a minimum.

Clearly the matter of clothes must be a personal choice. It should always be borne in mind that one is likely to get extremely dirty and may also damage clothes on nails or similar snags. Footwear should be similarly stout and weather-proof. Some industrial archaeologists prefer to carry boiler suits and wellington boots and change into these on arrival at the site. If it is not possible to carry the latter, then it is essential to wear old clothes. Remember, too, that many buildings are out of use or semi-derelict and unheated, so warm clothes or extra jerseys should be carried.

Perhaps the most important item of wearing apparel is the protective helmet, the 'hard-hat', made of plastic. These are available at builders' merchants at a cost of about £1 50p. Hard-hats are essential, for even if they are not required to protect the wearer from a serious accident, at least they help keep the hair clean. They should be strapped on so that they cannot be knocked off if the wearer falls.

Mention of serious accidents causes the author to sound his warning note on insurance. Industrial archaeology takes one into areas which can be derelict, or to buildings in which floors can suddenly collapse through rot: it is a hobby or profession which carries some risk. In the case of the amateur, an accident could immobilize him for quite a time. He should ensure that his accident insurance covers him for this sort of accident occurring in his spare-time hobby and provides for some form of salary maintenance if he is off work for any length of time. The author has had a minor accident which shows the extent to which care has to be taken. He was examining a horse wheel like the one at Mierscourt in Kent (Fig. 8). The horse arm was accidentally displaced which moved the upright slightly. This then fell away from the top bearing and crashed onto the author. The bottom bearing had settled into the ground so that it was only just held in the ring of the top bearing. It had looked quite safe! Similar situations are often met particularly as one is often working in dark buildings with only a torch for light. An industrial archaeologist working in the field on his own should take the precaution of leaving a note of his whereabouts before he leaves his home or hotel in the morning. A small first-aid kit or box containing necessary emergency items can deal with minor cuts and bruises on site.

What then constitutes a basic tool kit for the industrial archaeologist going to do survey work in the field? In the first place, each type of investigation carries its own requirements so, unless one has a van or shooting brake in which the tools can live permanently, thought should be given to the requirements before setting out.

For field records a hard-backed book with plain or lightly ruled squared paper is essential. This should be about 10 in. by 8 in. or of a size convenient for one's haversack or bag. HB or similar soft pencils, together with red and black ball-point pens and a rubber are needed for the recording in the field notebook.

A camera and photographic equipment, at least for working in black and white, are essential. However, Chapter 6 has already dealt with this aspect of fieldwork. It is, however, better that the photographic equipment is carried with the rest of the equipment in a haversack or bag than allowed to hang loosely on its own straps.

A large torch in a waterproof casing is also essential if the industrial archaeologist knows that he is going inside a building. Make sure before setting out that the batteries are fresh and will not let you down by failing at the wrong moment.

The measurement instruments are detailed in Chapter 5. At the least, a 2m (6-ft) measuring rod or flexible measuring tape should always be carried so that if one finds an object whose size it would be useful to record one is not reduced to measuring it with hand spans, thumb lengths and feet placed end to end!

An industrial archaeologist should always carry a few items in his car which can be used for more detailed investigation of a site or object. A garden trowel and hard-bristled brush will enable one to clear an object of weeds and dirt in readiness for photography or measurement. If the course of a dried-up stream or leat is being surveyed then surveyor's poles are needed to mark the centre line.

Chalk and a reel of string are obvious additions to the haversack or bag because with these one can mark objects for photographs or set out straight lines for survey purposes in conjunction with survey rods. A few foolscap-size plastic bags are useful to carry dirty finds or protect equipment from damp.

One further item which might not occur to an industrial archaeologist is a plastic bag containing a damp sponge or face cloth and a small rough towel. Nothing is worse than embarking on a long return journey if one has not been able to wash one's hands and face.

Experience will show the industrial archaeologist how much equipment he needs to take into the field. He should remember what he would feel like if he discovered a horse wheel for raising ore out of a mine some three or four miles from where he left his camera and tape!

8. Private records of fieldwork

The industrial archaeologist in the field must make records of his work as he goes along. He may succeed in publishing the results of his field studies or be making these studies purely for his own enjoyment. However, though a fieldworker starts out on his studies as a hobby, he may become so involved that publication must result. Whatever his intention it is clear that he must keep some forms of records so that he can refer to them at a later date when he is developing his studies.

The first item necessary for the keeping of records is a field notebook. This should be a hard-backed book, small enough for either one's pocket or a haversack. This book should be regarded as a notebook to be scribbled in, dirtied or defaced. The field notebook should be no more than an extension of the fieldworker's memory. On returning home, the fieldworker should write up his notes into his record book, using the notes in his field notebook and his memory to fill in small details. This record book can take the form of a loose-leaf book, a hard-backed book or a card-index system. The author uses a series of hard-backed books in which various types of field studies can be entered. A similar series is used as the field record of drawings and measurements from which measured drawings are made.

In writing up the record book the fieldworker should adopt a standard pattern. Each page should have only one item of fieldwork on it or be a continuation of a previous item. Head the page with a precise name detailing the object and its location and below that give its parish location, its county and the National Grid reference number of the site. Follow this with a description of what has been found on site. Any machinery should be clearly noted with its location, use and power system. As far as possible, the machinery should be listed in accordance with the order in which the product was taken through the building. Sketches should be made showing the way the buildings are set out and the positions of the various items of machinery. The record book should also state what photographs have been taken of the site. The fieldworker should make sure that his notes are intelligible to others, so that he can show his records to other workers. It is not necessary to type the records but they should be set out in the systematic way described above.

The fieldworker is working in black-and-white film, with colour taken only if there is a lecturing commitment. In the first instance he will normally have the film developed and simple 'proof' enlargements made. If he is working in his own darkroom the prints will be uniform with a reasonable degree of enlargement control used to produce a good print. The field-worker who has to use 'D. & P.' shops will get a reasonable print of uniform size which he can use for his own photographic record as these are usually a little smaller than postcard size. As soon as possible the field-worker should mount his prints in albums so that each unit of work is kept to its own page or pages. Mounting with 'Cow Gum' or its equivalent is best as loose corners are very awkward and the photographs frequently drop out. Identify the prints in the album with neat lettering, or by typing on white labels such as 'Butterfly' labels and cutting the labels to size before sticking them into the album. The negatives should be stored in the transparent wallets in which they are delivered after development and these should be kept unit by unit in separate envelopes. Store these in a cool drawer so that they can be referred to as though they were in a filing cabinet.

In addition to the fieldworker's own record books, he should fill in the record card of the National Record of Industrial Monuments (NRIM). These record cards are available from The Council for British Archaeology, 8 St Andrew's Place, Regents Park, London NW1. For some industrial archaeologists they can form a good, ready-made filing system of their own work. The author regards the filling in of the record cards as one of the duties of the fieldworker at the end of his day's work in the field. Only by having a comprehensive national record of industrial sites can industrial archaeologists press for preservation on a satisfactory and informed scale.

Figures 27 and 28 show the two sides of an NRIM Industrial Archaeology Record Card. This is the card for the horse wheel of the horse-driven corn mill at Narr Lodge, Quernmore, near Lancaster mentioned in Chapter 1 and Plate 5. Figure 27 shows the face of the card; this is always filled in. The 'Nature of the Site' panel contains also the address of the horse wheel. The 'Ref. No.' panel is not filled in, as this is where the national card number is inserted by the Consultant. The 'Parish/Township' panel is important, as this is used for relating the find to the lists of buildings of architectural or historic interest made under the Planning Acts. The next panels are for the personal opinions and descriptions prepared by the recorder. The panel relating to 'Printed Manuscript or Photographic Records' should record the photographs which were taken at the visit and if measured drawings are to be made. The card should not be delayed while finding out if any manuscript or other documents exist. Figure 28 shows the reverse side of the card. This should be used only if there is positive information or details to be added to amplify what has been recorded on the face of the card. In the case of Narr Lodge, the reverse was used to record the known information about the wheel so that the users of the card could get some

E OF SITE (Factory, mine, etc.) HORSE WHEEL NARR LODGE			COUNTY LANCASHIRE		REF.No.
Reference or Location SD 515 594.	Industry FARM USES	Dating c 1775	Parish/Township QUERNMORE		Date of Report 4 - 9 - 1973

PTION: dimensions; present condition; architectural features etc. THE FARM AT NARR LODGE
AS AT SOME TIME THE CHURCH FARM. TITHE BARN LISTED.
UILDING ADJACENT TO FARMHOUSE ON WEST CONTAINS HORSE WHEEL.
IS WHEEL ONLY REMAINING. NOTE THIS IS CLEARLY NOT A
RESHING WHEEL BUT DROVE A MILL.

her remarks or photo/sketch may be recorded on the back)

nery and Fittings   NIL — LAY SHAFT SEVERED.

r of Demolition or Damage   NOT AT THE MOMENT.

ed, Manuscript or Photographic Records   BLACK & WHITE PHOTOS. MEASURED J.K. MAJOR.
LISTED GRADE III (HORSE WHEEL & BUILDINGS).

ter's name and address:- J. KENNETH MAJOR 2 ELDON ROAD READING RG1 4DH.	Return to:- J.K. MAJOR

tution or Society:-

. Industrial Archaeology Report Card.

OVER

27   Face of NRIM Industrial Archaeology Record Card filled in for horse
wheel at Narr Lodge, Quernmore

idea of the machine. A sketch is much more use in a situation like this.
Sizes were transferred from the field notebook so that the rough sizes could
be seen. The reader will note the conjectural restoration of the horse arm
and the fact that the lay shaft at high level has been cut.

28   Reverse side of NRIM Industrial Archaeology Record Card filled in
with sketch and notes on horse wheel at Narr Lodge

The NRIM cards should be filled in using black ink or a black ball-point pen. The reason for this is that the cards are copied for the National Monuments Record, the Consultant on Industrial Monuments and the Bath University Centre and ordinary ink, pencil and photographs are not well reproduced by 'Xerox'-type copiers. When the cards have been completed they should be returned to The Consultant on Industrial Monuments, The Centre for the Study of the History of Technology, Bath University, Claverton Down, Bath.

The fieldworker should not be afraid to fill in the NRIM card. The chance that a card has already been filled in for a certain site should not deter the recorder. The previous card may be much older and so the later information may be important if preservation is under discussion. Equally a 'site only' record should be made as this enables the whole pattern of an industry in an area to be seen from the cards. Some may be deterred by their inability to add a sketch. The Narr Lodge sketch is set up with faint pencil lines, which could be put on with a set square and ruler, before being inked in. What is important is that a legible record card should have been made for each site.

The industrial archaeologist will find himself collecting all sorts of cuttings, articles from magazines and photographs, because he will want to build up his own archives of material for use in the interpretation of the sites he has found when at work in the field. He will also collect material that he finds on sites where the industry has been closed down. Owners often have no realization of the importance of the papers belonging to their industrial unit and condemn a great deal of paper to the bonfire. Much of this must indeed be scrap but the industrial archaeologist should look out for diaries, day books, catalogues, letter headings and account books. These should be used—if the fieldworker is proceeding to publication— and then deposited in the local record office. Similarly the industrial archaeologist may find himself collecting artefacts to save them from the scrap yard. (The author's work on animal-powered machinery stems from his rescue of the horse wheel and pumps from Swallowfield Park to the south of Reading.) The industrial archaeologist should ensure that his material will be deposited in the right place in the event of his death, as an important collection could easily be destroyed through lack of knowledge on the part of his executors.

Industrial archaeologists as a whole are extremely co-operative and so the fieldworker should share the knowledge of his finds with others. Only by building up a knowledge of our complete industrial pattern can the future of the important items be ensured. The industrial archaeologist should be prepared to lend his material, protecting it if publication is certain, so that others may gain from his experience and finds.

9. Publications of the results of fieldwork

The industrial archaeologist will reach a point, in his particular unit of fieldwork, at which he feels that some form of publication should be undertaken. The scale of the fieldwork will dictate the form of publication and in this the less experienced person should seek the opinions of others in his local group. At one end of the scale the industrial archaeologist will need to publish his fieldwork in the form of a book and at the other the fieldwork will need no more than a note in the newsletter or bulletin of a local society or group. Publication can also mean giving a lecture to industrial archaeologist colleagues, or lecturing or broadcasting to a large and heterogeneous audience with no particular knowledge of the subject.

The newsletter or bulletin of a local society or group may be an irregular publication, used mainly to give information about the group's activities and usually having short notes about the fieldwork carried out by members of the group. It is often in the newsletter that the first information about a threat to an industrial building is given. A note of this type may be only about 500 words in length and the description must, therefore, be precise in giving details about where the building is, what it is and what is happening to it. Five hundred words is not much to play with, so it is probably best to write out what is to be described and then to reduce its size to an acceptable length in a summary. Examples of this type of short note can be seen in the 'Notes and News' pages of *Industrial Archaeology*. The following short note by the author appeared in *The Berkshire Archaeological Journal, Vol. 65*, together with a page of line drawings showing the plan, sections and elevations of the cupola furnace in question. The note was entitled 'A Berkshire Foundry'.

In the centre of Bucklebury (SU 552 710) a group of buildings surmounted by a fine chimney has been the home of a working foundry and blacksmith's shop since the early 18th century and possibly earlier. This site for a foundry is an unusual one, as it is three miles from the Kennet Navigation at Woolhampton over a high ridge, and this would have made the carriage of iron bars, pig iron and coal or coke difficult.

The group of buildings is now in use for light engineering, garage work and sheet metal work but these activities have not really affected the layout of the group. The river Pang forms the northern boundary of the site, though the cottage on the north bank of the stream was at one time attached to the foundry. The little lane connecting the cottage to the main street of the village separates the group into two parts. The range of buildings to the west contained the workshops associated with the woodworking and wheelwright part of the business. At the south end of this range there is still the tyring furnace and beside it the cast iron tyring plate, and to the north of this there are the open cart sheds and woodworking shops. The interior of these is so altered that the particular use of any one is not recognizable. On the back wall there are a·row of racks for the storage of metal bars which have been produced as flat bed castings and consist of uprights with hooked brackets cast on to the uprights.

The east range of buildings of the foundry forms the more important part of the site for there the whole history of the group is shown in the buildings. The building with diamond panes next to the river is the original smithy which has been absorbed into the foundry. Behind that, still bordering the stream, is a large workshop with a heavy truss roof, dated 1844. The workshop contained, at its western end, the hearths and benches associated with the smiths and engineers who made or repaired the agricultural machinery which was the mainstay of the foundry. To the south of this workshop there is a parallel building, which may be of the same date, which was the shop where pumps and engines were made or repaired. The metal-working lathes had very long beds for turning the cores of the pumps and engine parts. The south west corner of this shop was the engine house to which the chimney was attached. Some form of horizontal steam engine was put in to drive the lathes and other machinery. The chimney is dated 1876 and it is possible that the engine was installed at the same time. The two workshops are approximately fifteen feet wide and sixty feet long. In the centre of each main wall there is a full-height double door so that steam engines and other large vehicles could be taken in for repair. The windows of these workshops are made of cast iron and are marked with the foundry's name 'Hedges'.

To the east of the north workshop there is a small compartment which houses the two furnaces, and beyond that is the pattern shop and the pattern store. In the grounds there are further sheds which served as wood stores, stables and cart sheds. There is also a frame in which oxen were tethered when they were being shod. The most modern part of the complex is a little brick office block and washroom which serves the petrol pumps in the forecourt.

Day books exist for the smithy which date from 1736 to 1764. These books show the Hedges family, as the local smiths, repairing farm machinery, shoeing horses and serving the needs of quite a large community. This family owned the foundry until 1908. The records show several John Hedges and a Nathaniel Hedges in charge, but for a large part of the middle of the 19th century the firm was controlled by Sarah Hedges. In 1908 the firm was bought by the Kings and operated by them until taken over by the Whatley brothers in 1947.

The foundry side of the business started about 1820. This date is confirmed by dated castings on the churchyard railings of Bucklebury and Frilsham of 1827 and 1824 respectively. The last dated casting is a tombstone made in 1957 in Bucklebury churchyard though the points for mechanical rakes have been cast since then. Patterns covering the whole period of the foundry's production are stored in the loft over the pattern shop. This loft is a wild clutter of uncatalogued pieces from waterwheels to windows, and from tombstones to troughs. Many gear patterns lie around; these were all hand carved and not cut on a machine as was the case in large foundries.

The most important item in the foundry is the cupola furnace which was used until quite recently and which was without doubt the furnace which was the basis of the foundry's business when it first started casting. This cupola is a stave cupola, that is it is made up of cast iron segments built up and held together like the staves of a barrel. The eight staves stand about seven feet high and are mounted on a cast iron plate. The top carries a square cast iron box which is the base of the flue which projects four feet above the roof. The centre stave at the front has the small door hole through which the iron was tapped. The side stave has three tuyère holes through which the blast was introduced. There is no doubt about the age of this form of furnace for it is shown in mid-19th century textbooks on foundry work with the caption 'the old type of cupola furnace'. The second cupola at the foundry is quite a standard cupola furnace with a ring of tuyères and an all metal casing standing on four iron posts. At the end of the foundry's life this had long been abandoned in favour of the older one. The air to the tuyères of both furnaces was provided by a series of channels under the floor which were fed by a fan. The power for the fan was provided by the present waterwheel. This wheel is an undershot wheel cast in the foundry about 1875, for which the patterns still exist.

The products of the foundry can be found throughout the local area. Some can be tracked down from the day books which exist from the latter part of the 19th century. For instance, the pump which stands at SU 516 674 on the A4 in Thatcham was supplied to the Thatcham Guardians in the 1870s; also the fine large stepped pyramid tomb in

Hampstead Norris churchyard for the Lousley family in 1855 to which memorial plates were added up to 1962. The waterwheels at Woolhampton Mill, River Barn Marlston, and the Bucklebury Manor Farm mill were all built by the foundry. At River Barn and the Manor Farm the foundry produced an important form of farm mill with a single pair of millstones. From the patterns other castings can be traced back to Bucklebury; the railings at Hampstead Norris church which are not marked are none the less the work of the Hedges family.

This short note covers only a fraction of the work and recording which has been done on this important industrial monument. A scale model of the cupola has been built for the International Foundry Congress held in Brighton this year. Photographs have been taken to record the patterns produced by the foundry; the waterwheel and mill at River Barn have been recorded as measured drawings. Indeed the inhabitants of the Pang valley must be worried about all the people who peer at their railings, gateposts and garden troughs.

Quite clearly, a tremendous amount of work could be done on this site as is indicated in the last paragraph. The note was written when the foundry and its very important cupola furnace was first discovered by the author in 1964 but it was not published until 1970. Ideally there would need to be a great deal of background research carried out on the foundry's products and its customs and economy before a full-scale paper could be written for the *Journal*. The note starts with a description of the site of the foundry, then continues with a description of the buildings and the way in which they were built. The note continues with short descriptions of the ownership of the complex over its life of more than 200 years. The foundry's products are touched on and the prime exhibit—the cupola furnace—is then described in some detail. The penultimate paragraph deals with some of the identifiable products in the nearby villages. (The cupola furnace has been moved to the Blists Hill section of the Ironbridge Gorge Museum as it was felt that its future had to be assured.)

The same note on the foundry at Bucklebury prepared for a local newspaper would have to be couched in quite different terms. Instead of a title like 'A Berkshire Foundry', a caption such as 'Berkshire has country's oldest furnace' would be better. Newspaper writing needs to be chatty and 'punchy' in order to secure and hold the attention of the general reader. Usually, however the material for a newspaper is prepared by the industrial archaeologist and then written up by a professional journalist after discussion with the original author. In view of a journalist's deadlines, it is not always possible to see the article in draft and so one has to grin and bear it when the article appears in print with inaccuracies or misunderstandings.

A report on a building or industrial monument has often to be written so that a case can be made out for the preservation of the building or financial support for its repair sought. Here, though not strictly a publication, a great deal of care has to be taken with the preparation. As this type of report will probably be read by officials, councillors, trustees and professional assessors, the writing has to be more 'dead pan' than in an article and superlatives have to be ruthlessly cut out. The statement that such-and-such is the 'only', or the 'oldest', example in a given area is not going to help the case much if the report is presented to someone who knows of a second example or an older and finer one elsewhere. What is needed in a report is a plain statement of fact neatly and precisely written. When the author first became involved with Dowrich Mill in Devon, he reported on the mill and the possibility of the owners, Mr and Mrs Lee, proceeding with its preservation. The following report was the one made after this first visit.

Dowrich Mill, Crediton, Devon

National Grid Reference: SS 823 048

Dowrich Mill nestles against the steep hillside in the valley of the river Creedy about quarter of a mile from the old Dowrich manor house to which it originally belonged. The mill complex consists of the mill with the old barns and cart sheds as well as the site of the mill house grouped around the mill yard. The road to the mill crosses the river and then climbs across the face of the hill to go on to Dowrich House. Where the road passes the mill it is at first floor level, and it has passed over a tunnel containing the leat; it then branches to the mill yard and to Dowrich House. The whole site with its background of the wooded hill is both secluded and beautiful.

The mill is built of stone, but it was extended to the south with cobb walls at a later date. The roof is made of slates on early timber trusses and rafters. The stone mill is rectangular and has been built into the hillside so that the first floor can be entered at road level by the gate to the mill yard, and at ground level at the south end. The yard slopes down across the mill so that the ground floor storey is half below ground on that side. On the opposite side, where the waterwheel is, the bank has been cut away so that the mill stands above ground, and the road is held up by a retaining wall. The walls of the mill are quite thick, and contain no windows on the side overlooking the stream. On the yard side in the main building there are windows at ground and first floor levels, and sack doors at ground and first floor levels in the cobb-walled extension. An access door exists in the main building on the wall facing the yard at the corner nearest to the entrance gate. In the gable overlooking the road in the main building there is a timber mullioned window of late 16th or early 17th century date.

The present mill equipment consists of the following items. There is an overshot waterwheel in a derelict state, which was fed with water from a wooden launder which reached from the pipe under the road to the wheel. This wheel has the remains of two cast iron rims 3·65 m (12′–0″) in diameter, with a cross section of 225 mm (9″) by 25 mm (1″) with cast slots to receive the 30 mm (1¼″) thick boards which formed the buckets. The whole of the inner face of the wheel, which is 1·30 m (4′–3″) wide, was boarded over with 30 mm (1¼″) boards. The six pieces of the rim were each supported by a wooden spoke socketed to the rim and to the cast iron hub. The hubs were supported on a 450 mm (18″) diameter wooden shaft, but this has decayed at the outer end.

The main shaft enters the mill and carries a pit wheel on its inner end. The pit wheel is made of iron and is 2·13 m (7′–0″) in diameter. This wheel is made up of a cast iron rim with 98 wooden teeth, which is bolted to the spokes. The wallower, which was driven by the pit wheel, is a single casting 900 mm (3′–0″) in diameter with 42 iron teeth. The cast iron great spur wheel which is 1·80 m (6′–0″) in diameter, is mounted on the upright shaft immediately above the wallower. This wheel is made up of a cast iron rim with 90 wooden teeth, which is bolted to the eight cast iron spokes. This in turn engaged with two cast iron stone nuts 450 mm (18″) in diameter. The stone nuts are mounted on rectangular iron stone spindles which drove the upper stones of the two pairs of millstones. The millstones are still in place on the stone floor. The 'upstream' pair are French stones supplied by Pearse of Exeter, and the 'downstream' pair are made of millstone grit. The tuns, hoppers and shoes are all missing from the mill.

The upright shaft continues past the stones and carries a cast iron crown wheel 1·22 m (4′–0″) in diameter with 60 wooden teeth. A lay shaft extends to the downstream wall at the end of the main building. This was driven by a 200 mm (8″) diameter cast iron bevel wheel. The lay shaft carried a series of pulleys to drive other machinery, all of which is now no longer there. The pulleys are all made of wood, and, in order outwards from the crown wheel, are 380 mm (15″) in diameter, 150 mm (6″) in diameter, 760 mm (30″) in diameter, 760 mm (30″) in diameter, and the final sack hoist pulley is 300 mm (12″) in diameter for use with a rope drive. The sack hoist was driven by a slack rope drive and remains on the attic floor. There were no storage bins of any sort on the top floor.

There is certain evidence in Dowrich Mill which gives a clue to the age of this mill and its site. Dowrich House is itself old, and the mill has clearly been associated with the farm of Dowrich House for a very long time. The leat, which has been dug out of the side of the hill, was a work of huge proportions, because it stretches back about half a mile to the site of a dam on the river Creedy. However, in the arrangement of the mill there are further clues to its age. In the wall beside the water-wheel there are two blocked up holes at low level, which, from their size and position, will have been holes for waterwheel shafts. Inside the mill, the pit wheel pit stretches the whole length of the wheel wall, and is protected by a low plinth on which a double hurst frame once stood, for two sets of gears and stones. It is unusual for a hurst frame, such as the present one, to be unsupported, and to bridge the wheel pit in this way. On the upper floor there are two long slots in the wall which were probably the hatch controls for the two original waterwheels. The roof trusses and the window in the gable wall could well be work of the late 16th or early 17th century. The arrangement of an attic floor without grain bins implies, but does not necessarily confirm, the use of the mill for toll milling as opposed to trading. Though the present millwork is typical of the work of Bodleys of Exeter in the 1870s, the importance of the mill lies in its previous history and its place in the history of mill-ing. To have such a long leat and an arrangement of millstones which was probably one pair of stones to each of two waterwheels, is indicative of a mill built at the end of the Middle Ages.

You will note that the above report follows the same pattern as that of the foundry note. One difference is evident here in the last paragraph. This has been written to give some evidence of the age of the mill and what could be concluded from this evidence. Reference back to the drawings and photo-graphs in Chapter 5 will give the reader some idea of the various items to which the author has drawn his attention. One further point in the pre-paration of a report is that the name and address of the author should be clearly stated at the end. These reports are often used for a number of different purposes: committee meetings, grant applications, etc. It is there-fore important that authorship is known.

Both the preceding examples are devoted to the description of individual units. The following article by Lawrence Cameron, 'Water Power Sites in Glenbuchat', is a study of a small area near Aberdeen.

The most northerly of the two rivers which find their way into The North Sea at Aberdeen is the River Don. The Don rises in the mountains to the west of Cock Bridge and flows through the widening valley of Strathdon until it reaches the broader Howe of Alford. The mill sites referred to are all situated in the valleys of the Buchat Water and the Kindie Burn which flow into the Don from the north between Cock

Bridge and Kildrummie. The area lies in the foothills of the Grampian Mountains, known locally as the Ladder Hills. The area was, and still is, a community of scattered crofting settlements at an elevation of some 450m (1500 ft) or more above sea level. The staple grain crop of the area had been oats, the area being too high and the climate too wet and uncertain for wheat.

It had been previously noted that within the Strathdon area there seemed to be an inordinate number of water power sites on which physical remains could be found. A history of the area, written in 1901 and published by the Spalding Society for Aberdeen Grammar School Library in 1928, however, recorded comparatively few mills. Three were said to exist in Strathdon Parish and only two, both of which were said to be disused in 1901, in the Parish of Glenbuchat. (The Parish of Glenbuchat included Glenkindie.) There was also said to be a 'Waukmill' at Glenkindie.

This field study was undertaken during a short holiday in the area and time precluded an extended survey so that it was decided to concentrate on sites in the Glenbuchat/Glenkindie area. The two corn mills referred to in the history were easily located at Milltown of Glenbuchat, NJ 367 167, and at Glenkindie, NJ 429 145. Surprisingly the latter was found to have been in use as a toll mill, serving the Glenkindie estates, as recently as 1970, and still to be in use as a saw mill. The saw mill is now driven by electricity, but water power was used until the closure of the corn mill in 1970. The mill was rebuilt following a fire in 1900 so that it may very well have been idle when the history of the Glen was written.

The present miller's father, Alec Reach, was responsible, as a millwright, for the rebuilding in conjunction with one Willie Ross who may have been the miller at that period. Much of the original mill machinery was retained during the rebuilding, but the mill building was enlarged by the addition of an extra floor and the wheel was replaced by a more modern overshot type of iron construction driving the original shaft via a spur gear. It is likely that the original wheel was of the modified alpine type, common in the area, in which a leat at high level feeds an undershot wheel having plain paddles via a downswept arrangement behind the wheel. This arrangement remains at Milltown of Glenbuchat which would seem to have been disused since about 1896. Internally the mills were similar having an iron shaft driving a cast pit wheel having wooden teeth. Drive to the twin stones being taken by lay shafts to left and right of the pit wheel with bevel gearing to the stone nuts. Other auxiliary machinery, lifts, sieves and sack hoist was driven by belting from the lay shafts.

Excluding the two corn mills, no trace was found of the waukmill, the sites located were similar in many respects. In every case wheel pits were found adjacent to steadings. The wheels appeared to have been between 3m (10 ft) and 4·60m (15 ft) in diameter and from 450mm (1 ft 6 in.) to 600mm (2 ft) in width. They all appear to have been undershot wheels, but of two distinct varieties. In the first, and arguably the earlier variety, the water was led to the base of the wheel by an underground leat. Examples of this type were found at Ryntaing, NJ 338 202, possibly the earliest of the sites examined, and at Newseat, NJ 344 195, both in Glenbuchat, and at Tollafraich, NJ 405 178, and at Largue, NJ 408 181, in Glenkindie. In what was, supposedly, a later type the water was led to the wheel at a higher level but a leat or launder usually of stone or concrete construction curved down behind the wheel to feed the paddles at low level. As previously indicated, this arrangement is quite common in the area on corn mills. This type was noted at Ballochduie, NJ 345 202, and at Easter Buchat, NJ 399 155, in Glenbuchat, and at Rinmore, NJ 416 171, in Glenkindie.

Apart from the two corn mills only one of the sites actually drew water from an already existing stream. At Largue, NJ 408 181, a short leat from the Kindie Burn fed the undershot wheel. The other sites, without exception, were fed from stone lined cisterns which gathered water from the steep hill sides by means of shallow artificial channels. The high rainfall and the saturated nature of the ground providing sufficient supply. These leats were generally 640m to 910m (700 to 1000 yards) in length. These kind of water arrangements would suggest that the works and the mills they served post dated the original settlements.

Given the frequency with which these mills occur it became obvious that they were associated with the needs of the upland crofts to which they were attached, and at Ballechduie, NJ 345 202, while the wheel had been removed, a small thrashing machine remained in situ. This had obviously been driven by the water wheel. Further enquiries of the farmers in the area confirmed that this had been so. The area was too remote, the roads too difficult, and the yield from these upland farms too meagre to allow of the practice of hiring a thrashing machine from a contractor.

This type of thrashing machine was the invention, in the late 1770s, of Andrew Meikle, an East Lothian millwright who had the distinction of employing the great engineer John Rennie as an apprentice for a period. According to the history of Glenbuchat, quoted earlier, these fan machines were adopted slowly in the area, the original practice of flailing and winnowing died hard, and steadings were arranged to make use of the prevailing wind in this respect. It is reported, however, that, once adopted, these machines remained in occasional use until the almost universal adoption of the combine harvester, within the last ten or twelve years. A horse wheel for the same purpose is recorded at Belnaboth, NJ 376 159, but appears to have been the only one in the area.

The steadings were, with only one exception (Largue, NJ 408 181, in Glenkindie) built into the hillside, and with minor exceptions were built with a main block at right angles to the slope of the hill and with two shorter wings, one at each end, forming a letter E with the centre arm removed. The harvested corn would be stored in the loft of the main building, which had ground level access on the uphill side, while stock would have been housed below. The loft would have been open to the upper level at the mill end, and the corn would have been fed from this level into the thrashing machine.

Outside the area under study, at Towmill, NJ 613 215, there is an example of this kind of installation which remains in working order. The building of rough stone construction, is, in this case in line with the slope of the hill rather than at right angles to it, and the floor is stepped. The wheel has a single iron frame in two parts mounted on an iron shaft. The wheel measures 3m (10 ft) by 450mm (1 ft 6 in.) carrying plain wooden paddles and is fed by a downswept concrete leat of the type described earlier. The wheel drives directly on to the machine shaft, there being no external gearing. The maker's name appears neither on the wheel nor on the machine itself.

Dating these sites is difficult, but bearing in mind that this type of thrashing machine did not come into general use until 1800 or a little later, and the recorded reluctance of the farmers of the area to adopt the innovation, it is perhaps reasonable to suppose that the earliest installations can not be earlier than about 1820, and that later installations of the downswept type probably date from about 1870 onwards.

Whether this kind of pattern is widespread in hill areas such as this in the North East of Scotland must be a matter for further research. The choice of water rather than animal power might reflect the relative poverty of the farms in this area, and also, to some extent, the predilections of the local landlord. (Farms in Glenshee, a very similar area to the south in Perthshire, would seem to have used animal power almost exclusively.) The ruins of these steadings are, in themselves, the visible expression of a changing pattern of land use in this relatively remote corner of North East Scotland.

List of Water Power Sites in Glenbuchat

Name of Site	Location	Function	Details etc.
Ryntaing	NJ 338 202	Thrashing	Ruined, wheel gone, 3·60m × 600mm (12′ × 2′)
Newseat	NJ 344 195	Thrashing	Abandoned, wheel gone, pit filled, possibly 3·60m (12′) diameter
Ballochduie	NJ 345 192	Thrashing	Abandoned, wheel gone, pit remains, downswept leat, thrashing machine in place
Balnacraig Milltown of Glenbuchat	NJ 367 167	Cornmill	Abandoned *c* 1896, wheel remains, iron on iron shaft 4·60m × 760mm (15′ × 2′6″), downswept launder, wooden paddles
Bridge of Buchat	NJ 400 156	Sawmill	Recorded *c* 1750, stone building remains, altered no trace of wheel or leat
Leochrie	NJ 399 180	Thrashing	Ruined, wheel gone, wheel pit shows wheel was 3m × 600mm (10′ × 2′)
Tollafraich	NJ 405 178	Thrashing	Steading in use, wheel gone 3m × 600mm (10′ × 2′) approx., downswept launder
Largue	NJ 408 181	Thrashing	Ruined, wheel gone, wheel pit remains, leat from Kindie Burn, 3·6m × 600mm (12′ × 2′)
Rinmore	NJ 416 171	Thrashing	Steading in use, wheel gone, pit filled, dimensions unknown
Glenkindie	NJ 429 145	Corn & Sawmill	Iron wheel on iron shaft, 4·60 × 900mm (15′ × 3′), rim gear driving sawmill and cornmill
Easter Buchat	NJ 399 155	Thrashing	Wheel gone, pit remains, 3m × 450mm (10′ × 1′6″) approx., pond filled in 1970

This study was made because Lawrence Cameron had found some of these farm wheel sites on one holiday and wanted to understand more about them. The following year he made this serious study of all the sites in these two valleys and then wrote the above short paper, in order to put his findings before other interested mill enthusiasts. In presenting his material he has purposely kept descriptions to a minimum. The importance of the water-supply arrangements has been brought out in the writing. No complete arrangements of these farm wheels existed in the area, so he uses an adjacent site, Towmill, to demonstrate the validity of his findings. He uses a table to identify the wheels and the millwork on each site. This is a useful point in a paper of this type, for it enables one to plot the sites on the map, to make comparisons, or to go over the ground oneself.

The most ambitious form of publication is the book. The main point about the book is that it should be a complete, or nearly complete, study of an area of fieldwork which has not been published before. The author's own book, *The Mills of the Isle of Wight*, is typical of a book which is in the main the result of fieldwork. Of course there is a fair amount of background information in such a book but it is essentially a fieldwork study. Without the fieldwork such a book would be pointless.

Books take a considerable amount of time to write, and so it is really unwise to complete the whole work of a manuscript and illustrations without a publisher in mind, although this sometimes happens. In the field of industrial archaeology with its limited appeal, going from publisher to publisher would be a very unrewarding exercise. The better way of going about the search for a publisher would be to have a volume of photographs and drawings which demonstrated the validity of your fieldwork and to couple this with a synopsis of a proposed book before approaching publishers who have been recommended to you. Personal contact and personal recommendation count for a great deal when publishers are evaluating a potential book.

In the first instance, when the fieldwork has reached the point of publication in book form, the first analysis of the book's scope, its chapter headings and its aims should be set out. From that the synopsis, or, better still, the specification of the proposed book should be written. The specification should contain each chapter heading with a few words setting out what each chapter contains. At the same time, the requirements for illustrations and drawings appropriate to the book should be worked out. It should be known what illustrations will be required and then, after commitment on the part of the publisher, how many illustrations and drawings can be used. When the publisher has stated that he is prepared to publish the book, he will indicate what range of illustrations he can tolerate and how many words the book should aim for. In agreeing terms and completing the contract for the book, it should be ensured that enough time has been allowed for its writing and production.

Whether one is writing a short paper or a full-length book there are several rules which should be applied. If one is committed to a publisher one should obtain the publisher's own rules so that the book or paper conforms to his house style. In the case of the journal, *Industrial Archaeology*, these rules are available from the editor and will enable the process of production to be easier. If one has no publisher in mind, one should use *Hart's Rules for Compositors and Readers* published by the Oxford University Press. This book and a publisher's own house rules give all the peculiar little points which are to be imposed to give a readable book. Details such as the preferred spelling of certain words, how to express numbers, and many other points are dealt with. The first thing for which to aim is a consistent approach. All words should be dealt with in the same way. If 'waterwheel' is used as one word, this spelling should be retained throughout the book, and if it is expressed as 'water wheel' then it should remain so consistently. In industrial archaeology there are many such words and over the period of time which a book takes to write it is easy to forget which way a particular word was used. It is, therefore, useful to have a check list of such words to which you can refer for the chosen spelling or hyphenation at a glance.

The subject of the book will dictate the form that the chapters will take. However, the introduction should set out the scope of the book and the reasons behind its preparation. The chapters should aim to lead the reader through the proposition given in the introduction and the book should be rounded off in the final chapter. If a gazetteer is used this should follow the concluding chapter and be an independent unit. If the gazetteer refers to items which have been described or discussed in the main body of the text, an entry should still be made in the gazetteer. The reader does not want to be referred back to the main text when his purpose is to use the gazetteer. A short note in the gazetteer with the words 'This is more fully described on page ooo', is better than the laconic 'see page ooo'...

Since most industrial archaeologists are writing about their own fieldwork and about the excitement their finds have given them, this excitement should be expressed in the book.

Quite early in the experience of the industrial archaeologist he is likely to be asked to prepare a lecture on the work he has been doing in the field. If he is a member of a local society or of an adult education course, there will usually be a students' or members' evening when they can present a short talk, usually about 15 minutes in length, on the results of their work.

This gives an opportunity to present a small unit of fieldwork or an unfinished portion of a larger unit. Fellow students or members will make comments or ask questions which will enable the lecturer to develop his theme or expand it when further work is being prepared for a longer lecture or other form of publication. Making a contribution like this at an informal evening among fellow enthusiasts gives one an excellent training in presentation and helps overcome any initial shyness.

The full-length lecture can take two or three forms. The simplest is a lecture to a group or society, which, whilst generally knowledgeable, has no particular skills in or knowledge of industrial archaeology. One is often called upon to speak to the archaeological society which sponsors the local industrial archaeology group. Often, too, one can be invited to a local body, such as a civic society, where the same audience conditions exist. The lecture has therefore to be given in a much more general fashion. The second, in order of difficulty, is the lecture given to a group of industrial archaeologists. The most important type of lecture, and the one needing the greatest care, is the paper presented to a learned society.

All lecture preparation needs careful planning and the needs of the particular audience must be taken into account. The author makes it a rule never to use the same lecture twice. After each lecture he puts the lecture slides away and gets out a different set of slides for the next lecture on the same subject. In this way the lecturer remains fresh and it also ensures that members of the audience, who may have been to previous lectures, are not bored.

In preparing for the sympathetic but general audience, the lecturer should compose a basic lecture. The general theme should be developed from first principles: the historical and geographical background and the history of the particular industry. The finds made in the study which is the subject of the lecture should be described in a simple non-technical fashion and the lecture should be rounded off with a short summary and conclusions. If, for example, the lecturer is talking about his local canal network to the local civic society, he should give details of the dates of construction and the local Acts of Parliament and then describe the highlights of the existing remains of the network. In summarizing the lecture, he could, since he is talking to a civic society, make a plea for their assistance in seeking the preservation of certain items illustrated during the lecture. At a meeting like this it is amazing, sometimes, to realize how members of the audience, in spite of their obvious concern for the amenity in question, had not known the value of certain humdrum items.

A lecture to fellow industrial archaeologists will need to be planned to different criteria. Obviously the lecturer will not need to develop the historical background but he will be able to speak much more fully on his subject and the finds he has made and use technical terms—with care. The care necessary will depend on the lecturer's knowledge of his audience; technical terms should not, however, be used solely to impress. He should also be very careful not to talk over the heads of his group. The lecturer should summarize with some precision, explaining how his finds relate to the industry elsewhere and should also explain how he proposes to develop the subject from the basis of his lecture.

A lecture to a learned society, such as the Newcomen Society, is a much more formidable proposition. The lecture is called a 'paper' and what usually happens is that the lecturer writes out his paper which is then duplicated and circulated to the members of the society prior to the lecture. This enables the lecture to be properly developed and written out in readiness for eventual publication in the transactions of that society. The lecturer should arrive knowing that interested members will have read the paper and have prepared questions on various aspects of the paper. Accordingly he should not read the paper word for word but should develop the important points following the general pattern of the paper. People are not necessarily good at reading aloud and there is nothing more boring for an audience than that they should have read to them something which they have read already and of which they have copies. The care taken in preparing a paper will be reflected in the discussion which follows. A member of the audience may have prepared a short written question and sent it privately beforehand to the lecturer. Any such question should be read and the answer given during the discussion. Questions from the floor will usually be brief and answers should be given 'off the cuff' at the lecture. If the paper is printed with a summary of the discussion then the facts of the 'off the cuff' replies can be checked or confirmed for the finished published transactions. However, in the circumstances described above, it is usually courteous for the lecturer before he embarks on the production of the paper, to find out as much as he can about the requirements of the society: how long the printed material can be; how many slides can be projected and subsequently published; and how long the lecture should last.

Lectures on industrial archaeology and its related fieldwork rely a great deal on illustrations. The audience will remember the visual images and will attach their memory of the points made in a lecture to the visual impressions they have gained. Slides are, therefore, important and their use must be carefully controlled by the lecturer. He will, if he is a good industrial archaeologist, be working with black-and-white photography as his main recording medium. If he knows that there is the likelihood of his eventually being asked to lecture on his finds, he will use a second camera for colour-slide production. However, if he is not able to do this, it should not prevent him from accepting lecture commitments as excellent slides can be made in black and white from 35-mm negative stock by most 'D. and P.' photographic laboratories quite cheaply. If the lecturer has some colour slides he can well add to them by using black-and-white slides if he has only black-and-white negatives of particular details. The 'punch' of colour slides should not, however, be overlooked when considering one's ability to hold the attention of an audience. If the lecturer has documentary material, it is better to make slides of this than to rely on an epidiascope for its projection. Epidiascopes are too awkward to manipulate in a lecture and the heat generated can damage precious material. By using the system described in Chapter 6, the material can be copied on Agfa Dia-Direct reversed stock. This is a slow film which is used for making black-and-white slides in the same way as normal colour slides.

Slides are now rarely bound between glass. Originally, when slides were produced from black-and-white negatives on $3\frac{1}{4}$-in. square glass, the sensitive emulsion had to be protected by a second clear sheet of glass. The first makers of colour slides also had to bind their colour strips of 35-mm material in 9cm ($3\frac{1}{4}$-in.) square slides or in between 6cm × 6cm (2-in. by 2-in.) glasses. Colour positives are nearly always supplied and processed by the manufacturers and in about 1960 they began to return the slide material mounted in plastic 6cm × 6cm (2-in. by 2-in.) frames ready for projection. All the lecturer now has to do, on receipt of the frames from the processing laboratory, is to put the projectionist's 'spot' in the correct place and put his lecture slides together. The lecturer should make sure that all the slides for any one lecture are bound in the same way. Projectors are now often controlled from the rostrum by the lecturer and when the focus has been set, the whole group of slides can be projected without the focus having to be changed. When a lecturer has gained confidence and does not need to use a written-out lecture, he should have a numerical list of his proposed slides with him as a guide. This saves him having to stop when each slide is changed to find out which one has come onto the screen.

The most enjoyable lectures are those in which the lecturer's enthusiasm and knowledge come over clearly. The lecturer should keep his head up and speak to the back of the room so that he can be heard by all present. When he demonstrates from a slide with a pointer he should remember not to talk to the screen but should turn to face the audience. Lecturing is perhaps the most rewarding form of publication for the industrial archaeologist because the close contact with the audience is encouraging. With practice, it need not be a cause of either shyness or nervousness.

knowledge in an area which has seemingly been covered. Discoveries in the field must be written up for record purposes, even if they are not published, but publication ought to be the aim of the fieldworker so that others may see what the pattern is in areas other than their own and thus learn more about their own area, and also so that eventually a national study of an industry can be made. In the first instance, publication can be made at local level in newsletters, society bulletins and local studies. Later, publication can be achieved in national journals or in book form.

A preservation policy can only be formed when the pattern of an industry over a single administrative area or the country as a whole has been completed. Fieldwork by industrial archaeologists is making a great contribution to such a policy of preservation. The Department of the Environment is the body responsible for scheduling buildings under the Ancient Monuments Acts and for listing buildings under the Planning Acts. To aid the Department, the Research Committee on Industrial Archaeology of the Council for British Archaeology and its Advisory Panel prepare lists of recommendations for industrial monuments needing some form of protection. These recommendations are prepared in various ways. In some instances the Consultant on Industrial Monuments studies an area or a subject, such as steam pumps on water supply premises. Clearly he cannot prepare these lists unless he is helped by fieldworkers in various areas or subjects up and down the country. In other instances the inspectors of the Department go to see selected monuments worthy of listing, which have been brought to their attention by interested people. Unless the rate of fieldwork and investigation of industrial monuments is stepped up there will be a growing loss of industrial buildings of importance. Obviously not all buildings can be protected—the financial resources and numbers of interested local people would not be enough—but at least the selected ones must have all the protection that is available under government legislation.

The fieldworker should not work entirely in isolation. He may pursue his own chosen subject by himself but he should make contact with other industrial archaeologists by attending courses or joining local groups when these exist. A lot of information about these groups can be obtained from the current edition of *Industrial Archaeologists' Guide*. Only by meeting other industrial archaeologists will he broaden his own experience and be able to discuss his finds and understand them. At a national level in Britain there is the Association for Industrial Archaeology, which was formed in 1973. This, it is hoped, will become the co-ordinating body for industrial archaeological research, for publishing and for holding seminars. A similar body, the Society for Industrial Archeology was founded in the USA in 1972 with the same purpose. This Society brings out a regular newsletter and occasional publications and conducts several seminars, visits and 'walk-abouts' each year. Membership of such societies gives the industrial archaeologist an insight into what is going on in other areas and enables him to make contact with other workers.

Several societies exist in Britain for the study and preservation of the objects of particular industries. Railways have their own specialist groups —as do canals—but there are also societies for the study of windmills and watermills, stationary steam engines, farm machinery, metallurgy and mining. Information about these societies can be obtained from *Industrial Archaeologists' Guide*. Whilst there is, as yet, no international society for industrial archaeology, there is a great deal of interchange of information and students of industrial archaeology between one country and another. Some specialist societies have, however, formed themselves into international societies so that there can be an interchange of research material, ideas and knowledge between one country and another.

Industrial archaeology has a considerable amount to give now and in the future. The fieldworker studying sites in his own area can make a significant contribution to the pattern of industrial monuments and by careful recording can ensure that a complete picture is built up of our industrial past. Losses of some of our industrial buildings must be inevitable, so it is up to the industrial archaeologist to see that they are recorded before they are lost. When preservation is accepted the fieldworker's knowledge can help to make that preservation more complete and accurate.

Bibliography

This list of books has been prepared to give the fieldworker in industrial archaeology an insight into the subject as a whole and into the various books in which good fieldwork in recorded. When he is at work in the field, the industrial archaeologist may find items of industrial machinery and remains which need further exploration, or which need to be related to other examples of similar machines or buildings. In order to enable the fieldworker to identify machinery or buildings some of the volumes which may help him in this way have been listed under fairly general headings.

There is a wealth of Victorian textbooks of machinery which can often be brought quite cheaply in secondhand book shops and the dedicated industrial archaeologist should be on the lookout for such volumes as they are an important aid to interpretation. Similarly valuable are the books which were published in the first half of this century such as *The Children's Encyclopedia* or the various volumes of *The Wonder Book for Boys*, for these well-illustrated books give an idea of the industrial practices in use at the turn of the century, most of which are now out of date.

General books on industrial archaeology

Bracegirdle, Brian *The Archaeology of the Industrial Revolution* (1973).

Buchanan, R. A. *Industrial Archaeology in Britain* (1972).

Buchanan, R. A. (ed.) *The Theory and Practice of Industrial Archaeology* (1968).

Cossons, Neil and Hudson, Kenneth *Industrial Archaeologists' Guide* (1971), published biennially.

Hudson, Kenneth *Handbook for Industrial Archaeologists* (1967).

Hudson, Kenneth *Industrial Archaeology, an Introduction* (2nd edition 1966).

Hudson, Kenneth *A Guide to the Industrial Archaeology of Europe* (1971).

Pannell, J. P. M. (ed. Major, J. K.) *The Techniques of Industrial Archaeology* (2nd edition 1974).

Raistrick, Arthur *Industrial Archaeology, an Historical Survey* (1972).

Richards, J. M. and De Mare, Eric *The Functional Tradition in Early Industrial Buildings* (1958).

Industrial archaeology—studies of particular areas and subjects

Ashmore, Owen *The Industrial Archaeology of Lancashire* (1969).

Banks, A. G. and Schofield, R. B. *Brindley at Wet Earth Colliery, an Engineering Study* (1968).

Bawden, Garrard, Qualtrough and Scatchard *The Industrial Archaeology of the Isle of Man* (1972).

Booker, Frank *The Industrial Archaeology of the Tamar Valley* (1967).

Branch Johnson, W. *The Industrial Archaeology of Hertfordshire* (1970).

Brunner, Hugo and Major, J. Kenneth *Water Raising by Animal Power* (1973).

Buchanan, Angus and Cossons, Neil *The Industrial Archaeology of the Bristol Region* (1969).

Buchanan, Angus *Bristol, Industrial History in Pictures* (1970).

Butt, John *The Industrial Archaeology of Scotland* (1967).

Butt, John, Donnachie, Ian and Hume, John R. *Scotland, Industrial History in Pictures* (1968).

Curnow, W. H. *Industrial Archaeology of Cornwall* (*c.* 1969).

Donnachie, Ian *The Industrial Archaeology of Galloway* (1971).

Day, Joan *Bristol Brass, The History of the Industry* (1973).

Enfield Archaeological Society *Industrial Archaeology in Enfield* (1971).

Green, E. R. R. *The Industrial Archaeology of County Down* (1963).

Harris, Helen *The Industrial Archaeology of Dartmoor* (1968).

Harris, Helen *The Industrial Archaeology of the Peak District* (1970).

Hudson, Kenneth *The Industrial Archaeology of Southern England* (1965).

Marshall, J. D. and Davies-Shiel, M. *The Industrial Archaeology of the Lake Counties* (1969).

Marshall, J. D. and Davies-Shiel, M. *The Lake District at Work* (1971).

Nixon, Frank *The Industrial Archaeology of Derbyshire* (1969).

Smith, David M. *The Industrial Archaeology of the East Midlands* (1965).

Todd, A. C. and Laws, Peter *The Industrial Archaeology of Cornwall* (1972).

Trinder, Barrie *The Industrial Revolution in Shropshire* (1973).

Vogel, Robert M. *A Report of the Mohawk–Hudson Area Survey* (1973).

Wilson, Aubrey *London's Industrial Heritage* (1967).

Agriculture

Darby, H. C. *The Draining of the Fens* (1940).

Higgs, John *The Land* (1964).

Hughes, W. J. *A Century of Traction Engines* (1971).

Wood, Emma and Hawke, Peter *Our Agricultural Heritage—A Selection of Farm Machinery Restored* (1971).

Building

Arkell, W. J. *Oxford Stone* (1947).
Barley, M. W. *The House and Home* (1963).
Barley, M. W. *The English Farmhouse and Cottage* (1961).
Brunskill. R. W. *Illustrated Handbook of Vernacular Architecture* (1970).
Peate, Iorwerth C. *The Welsh House* (1940).
Searle, Alfred S. *Modern Brickmaking* (1911).
Smith, J. T. and Yates, E. M. *The Dating of English Houses from External Evidence*, reprinted from *Field Studies* vol. 2, No. 3, (1968).
Tann, Jennifer *The Development of the Factory* (1970).

Canals and navigable rivers

Clew, Kenneth R. *The Kennet and Avon Canal* (1968).
De Mare, Eric *The Canals of England* (1950).
De Salis, H. R. *Bradshaw's Canals and Navigable Rivers of England and Wales* (1904) reprint (1969).
Hadfield, Charles *British Canals, an Illustrated History* (1950).
Hadfield, Charles *The Canals of South Wales and the Border* (1960).
Hadfield, Charles *The Canals of South and South East England* (1969).
Hadfield, Charles *The Canals of South West England* (1967).
Harris, Robert *Canals and Their Architecture* (1969).
Household, Humphrey *The Thames and Severn Canal* (1969).
Vine, P. A. L. *London's Lost Route to the Sea* (1965).
Vine, P. A. L. *London's Lost Route to Basingstoke* (1968).

Civil engineering—roads, bridges etc.

Berridge, P. S. A. *The Girder Bridge after Brunel and Others* (1969).
Crosby, Theo. *The Necessary Monument* (Tower Bridge) (1970).
De Mare, Eric *Bridges of Britain* (1954).
Hopkins, H. J. *A Span of Bridges* (1970).
Pannell, J. P. M. *An Illustrated History of Civil Engineering* (1964).
Straub, Hans *A History of Civil Engineering* (1952).

Industrial history

Ashton, T. S. *The Industrial Revolution, 1760–1830* (1970).
Burstall, Aubrey F. *A History of Mechanical Engineering* (1963).
Challoner, W. H. and Masson, A. E. *Industry and Technology* (1963).
Chapman, S.D., Chambers, J. D. and Sharpe, T. R. *The Beginnings of Industrial Britain* (1970).

Derry, T. K. and Williams, Trevor I. *A Short History of Technology* (1960).

Mechanical Engineers, Institute of *Engineering Heritage, Highlights from the History of Mechanical Engineering* (1963 and 1966).

Quennell, Marjorie and C. H. B. *A History of Everyday Things in England,* 4 vols. (1934).

Rolt, L. T. C. *Tools for the Job* (1965).

Singer, Charles and others *A History of Technology,* 5 vols. (1954–58).

Tomlinson, Charles *Cyclopaedia of Useful Arts, Manufacturers, Mining and Engineering,* 2 vols. (1854).

Wilson, Mitchell *American Science and Inventions, A Pictorial History* (1960).

Local history and associated studies

Beresford, M. W. and Joseph, J. K. S. *Mediaeval England, an Aerial Survey* (1958).

Bond, Maurice *The Records of Parliament* (1964).

Crawford, O. G. S. *Archaeology in the Field* (1953).

Hoskins, W. G. *Local History in England* (1959).

Hoskins, W. G. *Making of the English Landscape* (1963).

Hoskins, W. G. *Fieldwork in Local History* (1967).

Metals

Clough, Robert T. *The Lead Smelting Mills of the Yorkshire Dales* (1962).

Gale, W. K. V. *The British Iron and Steel Industry* (1967).

Gale, W. K. V. *The Black Country Iron Industry* (1966).

Hofman, H. O. *The Metallurgy of Lead* (1899).

Straker, Ernest *Wealden Iron* (1931) reprint (1967).

Turner, Thomas *The Metallurgy of Iron* (1895).

Mining

Agricola, Georgius *De Re Metallica* (1556), translated Herbert Hoover and reprinted (1950).

Atkinson, Frank *The Great Northern Coalfield 1700–1900* (1966).

Barton, D. B. *A History of Copper Mining in Cornwall and Devon* (1968).

Barton, D. B. *Essays in Cornish Mining History* (1968).

Down, C. G. and Warrington, A. J. *The History of the Somerset Coalfield* (1971).

Earl, Bryan *Cornish Mining* (1968).

Hughes, Herbert W. *A. Text-book of Coal Mining* (1893).

Kirkham, Nellie *Derbyshire Lead Mining* (1968).
Morgan Rees, D. *Mines, Mills and Furnaces* (1969).
North, F. J. *Mining for Metals in Wales*, Nat. Museum of Wales (1962).
Shaw, W. T. *Mining in the Lake Counties* (1972).

Photography

Allsopp, Bruce and Clarke, Ursula *Photography for Tourists* (1966).
Becher, Bernard and Hilda *Anonyme Skulpturen, Eine Typologie Technischer Bauten* (1970).
De Mare, Eric *Photography and Architecture* (1961).
De Mare, Eric *Colour Photography* (1968).
De Mare, Eric *Photography* (1957).
Matthews, S. K. *Photography in Archaeology and Art* (1969).
Simmons, Harold C. *Archaeological Photography* (1969).

Power

Barton, D. B. *The Cornish Beam Engine* (1965).
Dickinson, H. W. *A Short History of the Steam Engine* (1938) reprint (1963).
Jamieson, Andrew *A Text Book of Steam and Steam Engines* (1886).
Lewis, Paul *The Romance of Water Power* (c. 1930).
Rankine, Prof. W. J. M. *A Manual of the Steam Engine and Other Prime Movers* (1859).
Watkins, George *The Stationary Steam Engine* (1968).
Watkins, George *The Textile Mill Engine* 2 vols. (1970).

Railways

Baxter, Bertram *Stone Blocks and Iron Rails* (1966).
Coleman, Terry *The Railway Navvies* (1966).
Dendy Marshall, C. F. *A History of British Railways down to the year 1830* (1938) reprint (1971).
Lewis, M. J. T. *Early Wooden Railways* (1970).
Meeks, Carroll V. *The Railway Station* (1956).
Smithson, A. and P. *The Euston Arch* (1968).
Snell, J. B. *Mechanical Engineering; Railways* (1971).
Tomlinson, W. W. *North Eastern Railway, its Rise and Development* (1914) reprint (1967).

Rural crafts and minor industries

Arnold, James *The Shell Book of Country Crafts* (1968).
Hartley, Dorothy *The Countryman's England* (2nd edition 1942).
Hennell, Thomas *The Countryman at Work* (1947).
Jenkins, J. Geraint *Traditional Country Craftsmen* (1965).
Pullbrook, Ernest C. *English Country Life and Work* (1922).
Rose, Walter *The Village Carpenter* (1937).
Sturt, George *The Wheelwright's Shop* (1923) reprint (1963).
Wymer, Norman *English Country Crafts* (1946).
Wymer, Norman *English Town Crafts* (1949).

Watermills and windmills

Armengarde (Aine) *Moteurs Hydralique vol. I text, vol. II Atlas Hydralique* (1868).
Batten, M. I. *English Windmills* vol. I (1932).
Bennett, Richard and Elton, John *History of Cornmilling*, 4 vols. (1899)—the more important vol. II was reprinted (1973).
Coles Finch, W. *Watermills and Windmills* (the windmills of Kent) (1933).
Farries, K. G. and Mason, M. T. *The Windmills of Surrey and Inner London* (1966).
Freese, Stanley *Windmills and Millwrighting* (2nd edition 1971).
Hills, R. L. *Machines, Mills and Uncountable Costly Necessities* (1967).
Jespersen, Anders (ed.) *Report on Watermills vol 3* (a large volume of measured drawings) (1957).
Major, J. Kenneth *The Mills of the Isle of Wight* (1970).
Reynolds, John *Windmills and Watermills* (1970).
Short, Michael *Windmills in Lambeth, an Historical Survey*, London Borough of Lambeth (1971).
Skilton, C. P. *British Windmills and Watermills* (1947).
Smith, Donald *English Windmills*, vol. II (1932).
Somervell, John *Water-Power Mills of South Westmorland* (1930).
Tann, Jennifer *Gloucestershire Woollen Mills* (1967).
Wailes, Rex *The English Windmill* (2nd edition 1967).
Wailes, Rex *Windmills in England* (1948).
Wolff, Alfred R. *The Windmill as Prime Mover* (2nd edition 1894).

Journals

The dedicated industrial archaeologist will normally subscribe to the journal *Industrial Archaeology*. This journal, which appears quarterly, carries articles on the full range of the subject. Articles are presented on fieldwork results, on various aspects of research and on the activities of various groups in the fields of preservation and recording.

Local groups produce their own newsletters, bulletins or magazines. The quality naturally varies according to the size of the group's membership and its method of distribution. The more notable of these local publications are *The Newsletter of the Gloucestershire Society of Industrial Archaeology*, *Sussex Industrial History*, *Industrial Archaeology in Wales Newsletter* and *Wiltshire Industrial Archaeology*. Details of these and similar publications can be found in the *Industrial Archaeologists' Guide*, which appears biennially.

The *Transactions* of the Newcomen Society are a further valuable source of material in the fields of industrial archaeology and industrial history. The Newcomen Society for the study of the history of engineering and technology has its headquarters at the Science Museum, London SW7. Since the society was founded, some 40 volumes of the transactions have been published and these contain a great number of authoritative and original papers on all aspects of industrial history. Fieldworkers should look for the papers of Mr Rex Wailes because these are studies of particular aspects of windmills and watermills built up by field studies over a lifetime of enthusiastic recording and are models of systematic documentation. As membership of the Newcomen Society is the same as the cost of the transactions—£6 per annum in 1973—joining the society is a step some industrial archaeologists may wish to take.

Some fieldwork may need background research to identify lost sites. Good sources of information are the back numbers of *Country Life* and *The Countryman* and also the local topographical magazines—of which *Hertfordshire Countryside* is an example.

Index